Song of Mind

Books by Chan Master Sheng Yen

Song of Mind

Wisdom from the
Zen Classic *Xin Ming*

■ · · · ■

Chan Master Sheng Yen

Shambhala
Boston & London ■ 2004

Shambhala Publications, Inc.
Horticultural Hall
300 Massachusetts Avenue
Boston, Massachusetts 02115
www.shambhala.com

Printed in the United States of America

∞ This edition is printed on acid-free paper that meets the American
National Standards Institute z39.48 Standard.
♻ Shambhala Publications makes every effort to print on recycled
paper. For more information please visit www.shambhala.com.

Distributed in the United States by Penguin Random House LLC
and in Canada by Random House of Canada Ltd

Interior design and composition: Greta D. Sibley & Associates

Library of Congress Cataloging-in-Publication Data
Shengyan, 1930–
Song of mind: wisdom from the Zen classic Xin ming/Chan Master
Sheng Yen.—1st ed.
p. cm.
ISBN 978-1-59030-140-1 (pbk.: alk. paper)
1. Zen Buddhism—Doctrines. 2. Enlightenment (Zen Buddhism)
3. Meditation—Zen Buddhism. 4. Niutoufarong, 594–657. Xin
ming. I. Title: Wisdom from the Zen classic Xin ming. II. Title.
BQ9268.7.S55 2004
294.3'4—DC22
2004008834

Contents

Acknowledgements

The Dharma lectures on Chan master Niutou Farong's *Song of Mind* that constitute the material for this book were given during several seven-day Chan retreats in America. Many people have contributed to it, beginning with the students and disciples who attended the retreats, thus providing me with the causes and conditions for my words of exhortation and encouragement.

I also want to thank members of the sangha as well as volunteers who assisted in the organization and presentation of the retreats, not the least of whom included those who prepared healthy vegetarian fare for the participants three times a day.

In addition, I am grateful to several other people for their specialized skills in putting together the final manuscript of *Song of Mind*, the first of whom were the Chinese-to-English translators who rendered my remarks into English as I spoke. The talks were recorded on cassette tapes, transcribed digitally, and edited for publication. For their contribution I would like to acknowledge the following people:

Translation: Ming Yee Wang, Paul Kennedy
Transcribing: Christine Sha, Anselma Rodgrigues, Bruce
    Rickenbacher
Editing: Ernest Heau, Chris Marano
Editorial assistance: Stacey Polacco, Mike Morical, Wei-tan
Publication: Iris Wang

Finally, I want to thank Shambhala Publications for issuing this edition, which allows the great Chan master Niutou Farong to reach out across many centuries to share his wisdom with practitioners today who continue to seek and practice the Way.

Sheng Yen
New York City, 2004

Song of Mind

Introduction

Master Niutou Farong (594–657) was a disciple of the fourth patriarch of Chan Buddhism, Dayi Daoxin (580–651). Niutou was also a Dharma brother of the fifth patriarch, Daman Hongren (602–675). According to Chan records, after Niutou left home to become a monk, he first studied Buddhist theory with a scholar of the Sanlun (Three Treatise) School. In addition, he was well versed in Confucian and Daoist philosophy and ritual, Chinese history, as well as the medical arts. However, Niutou favored Chan meditation most of all, and spent twenty years practicing deep in a mountain forest, where he befriended the wild animals. When Patriarch Daoxin heard of the monk and his practice, he went to guide Niutou. After becoming enlightened under Daoxin, Niutou attracted disciples of his own, acquiring over three hundred followers. Niutou lectured mostly on the *Lotus Sutra* and the *Prajnaparamita Sutra*. He also studied the *Vimalakirti Sutra* and the *Avatamsaka Sutra*, the latter being the basis of the Huayan School of Chan.

In his poem *Song of Mind*, Niutou explains that our mind is originally pure, but when even one thought enters the mind, its purity is lost. He therefore placed great importance on a method of practice, which is to watch our thoughts arising and falling. But the rise and fall (literally, birth and death) of thoughts is illusory, because if the present thought remains unmoving, and does not disappear, then a succeeding thought will not arise. At this point there is neither arising nor falling of thoughts. Therefore, there is nothing to cut off. Thus, Niutou says that while buddhas and sentient beings originally have no mind, mind comes about because we have thoughts. For sentient beings to attain buddhahood, their illusory mind must become no-mind, that is to say, become enlightened.

Niutou's method emphasizes cultivating wakefulness (*hsing*) and stillness (*chi*) together without attaching to either. In the beginning we must use our senses to observe the world, but we should not use discriminating mind to attach to the world. When we let go of discrimination, the illusory world that is presented to our senses will recede and disappear. Along with the vanishing of the illusory world, our ordinary mind also vanishes and we experience pure, or original, mind.

Having reached that point, the enlightened mind still functions normally in the world. In fact, others will see you as an ordinary person. The difference is that your mind is not moving, not discriminating. Therefore, the *Song of Mind* says that true enlightenment is no enlightenment, and true emptiness is not empty. Without leaving this true emptiness, you can still practice and espouse the Dharma. However you are now not practicing to become a buddha; practicing is just what you do. Ordinary people feel they need a reason to do something, but practicing with a goal in mind makes it impossible to get to the state of no-mind.

Song of Mind (Xin Ming)

by Niutou Farong (594–657)

The nature of the mind is non-arising,   I
What need is there of knowledge and views?
Originally there is not a single dharma;
Why discuss inspiration and training?

Coming and going without beginning;
Sought for, it is not seen.
No need to do anything;
It is bright, still, self-apparent.

The past is like empty space;
Know anything and the basic principle is lost.
Casting a clear light on the world,
Illuminating, yet obscured.

If one-mindedness is impeded,
All dharmas are misunderstood.
Coming and going thus,
Is there need for thorough investigation?

Arising without the mark of arising,
Arising and illumination are the same.

NOTE: The numbers in the right margin refer to the chapter that discusses that portion of the verse.

Desiring to purify the mind,
There is no mind for effort.

Throughout time and space nothing is   2
    illuminated;
This is most profound.
Knowing dharmas is non-knowing;
Non-knowing is knowing the essential.

Using the mind to maintain quietude,
You still fail to leave the sickness.
Birth and death forgotten—
This is original nature.

The highest principle cannot be explained;
It is neither free nor bound.
Lively and attuned to everything,
It is always right before you.

There is nothing in front of you;   3
Nothing, yet everything is as usual.
Do not belabor wisdom to examine it;
Substance itself is empty and obscure.

Thoughts arise and pass away,
The preceding no different from the succeeding.
If the succeeding thought does not arise,
The preceding thought cuts itself off.

In past, present and future, there is nothing;
No mind, no buddha.
Sentient beings are without mind;
Out of no-mind they manifest.

Distinguishing between profane and sacred,
Their vexations flourish.
Splitting hairs deviates from the eternal.
Seeking the real, you give up the true.

Discarding both is the cure,
Transparent, bright, pure.
No need for hard work or skill;
Keep to the actions of an infant.

4

Clearly knowing,
The net of views increases
Stillness without seeing,
Not moving in a dark room.

Wakeful without wandering,
The mind is tranquil yet bright.
All phenomena are real and eternal,
Profuse, yet of a single form.

Going, coming, sitting, standing,
Don't attach to anything.
Affirming no direction,
Can there be leaving and entering?

There is neither unifying nor dispersing,
Neither slow nor quick.
Brightness and tranquillity are just as they are.
They cannot be explained in words.

5

Mind is without alienation;
No need to terminate lust.
Nature being empty, lust will depart by itself.
Allow the mind to float and sink.

Neither clear nor clouded,
Neither shallow nor deep.
Originally it was not ancient;
At present it is not modern.

Now it is non-abiding;
Now it is original mind.
Originally it did not exist;
"Origin" is the present moment.

Bodhi has always existed;
No need to preserve it.
Vexation has never existed;
No need to eliminate it.

Natural wisdom is self-illuminating;
All dharmas return to thusness.
There is no returning, no receiving;
Stop contemplating, forget keeping.

The four virtues are unborn;
The three bodies have always existed.
The six sense organs contact their realms;
Discrimination is not consciousness.

In one-mindedness there are no   6
    wandering thoughts,
The myriad conditions harmonize.
Mind and nature are intrinsically equal;
Together, yet one does not necessarily lead to
    the other.

Without arising, complying with phenomena,
Abiding hidden everywhere.

Enlightenment arises from non-enlightenment.
Enlightenment is non-enlightenment.

As to gain and loss,
Why call either good or bad?
Everything that is active
Originally was not created.

Know that mind is not mind;
There is no sickness, no medicine.
When in confusion, you must discard affairs;
Enlightened, it makes no difference.

Originally there is nothing to obtain;
Now what use is there in discarding?
When someone claims to see demons,
We may talk of emptiness, yet the phenomena
    are there.
Don't destroy the emotions of people;   7
Only teach the cessation of thoughts.

When thoughts are gone, mind is abolished;
When mind is gone, action is terminated.
No need to confirm emptiness;
Naturally, there is clear comprehension.

Completely extinguishing birth and death,
The profound mind enters into principle.
Opening your eyes and seeing forms,
Mind arises in accord with the environment.

Within mind there is no environment;   8
Within the environment there is no mind.

Use mind to extinguish the environment
And both will be disturbed.

With mind still and environment thus,
Not discarding, not grasping,
Environment is extinguished together with mind.
Mind disappears together with environment.

When neither arises,
There is tranquillity and limitless brightness.
The reflection of bodhi appears
In the eternally clear water of mind.

The nature of merit is like a simpleton:
It does not establish closeness and distance.
Favor and disgrace do not change it;   9
It doesn't choose its abode.

All connections suddenly cease;
Everything is forgotten.
Eternal day is like night,
Eternal night, like day.

Outwardly like a complete fool,
Inwardly mind is empty and real.
Those not moved by the environment
Are strong and great.

There are neither people nor seeing.   10
Without seeing there is constant appearance.
Completely penetrating everything,
It has always pervaded everywhere.

Thinking brings unclarity,
Sinking and confusing the spirit.

Use mind to stop activity
And it becomes even more erratic.

The ten thousand dharmas are everywhere,
Yet there is only one door.
Neither entering nor leaving,
Neither quiet nor noisy.

The wisdom of sravakas and pratyekabuddhas   11
Cannot explain it.
Actually there is not a single thing;
Only wonderful wisdom exists.

The original face is limitless;
It cannot be probed by mind.
True enlightenment is no enlightenment,
Real emptiness is not empty.

All buddhas of the past, present and future
All ride on this basic principle.
The tip of a hair of this basic principle
Contains worlds numerous as the Ganges sands.

Do not concern yourself with anything;   12
Fix the mind nowhere.
Fixing the mind nowhere,
Limitless brightness shows itself.

Tranquil and non-arising,
Set free in boundless time and space.
Whatever it does, there is no obstruction.
Going and staying are equal.

The sun of wisdom is tranquil,
The light of samadhi is bright.

Illuminating the garden of no forms,
Shining on the city of nirvana.

After all relationships are forgotten,
Spirit is understood and settled in substance.
Not rising from the Dharma seat,
Sleeping peacefully in a vacant room.

Taking pleasure in Dao is calming,
Wandering free and easy in reality.
No action and nothing to attain,
Relying on nothing, manifesting naturally.

The four unlimited minds and the six paramitas
Are all on the path of one vehicle.
If mind is not born,
Dharmas will not differ from one another.

Knowing arising is non-arising,
Eternity appears now.
Only the wise understand,
No words can explain enlightenment.

The nature of mind is non-arising

1.1 ■ Thoughts Are Illusory

> The nature of the mind is non-arising,
> What need is there of knowledge and views?

Niutou's opening line, *The nature of the mind is non-arising*, is what the Buddha himself taught—that all thoughts are illusory. People on retreat are often concerned with sleepiness and scattered mind. However, these thoughts come and go; they were not originally present in the mind, nor are they ever-present. Thus we call them illusions, for Buddhism considers all temporal phenomena to be illusory. If scattered mind were not illusory, it would always be present, and it would never change; if sleepiness were not a temporal phenomenon, you would be sleepy all the time. The fact is that when the mind is concentrated, scattering disappears, and when it is awake, drowsiness is gone. Therefore, sleepiness and scattered mind are both illusory. Meditation is also an illusion, but we use it to help the illusory mind to cease arising.

To come to retreat expecting to get enlightened, to experience buddha-mind, is self-deception. Indeed, since there is no such thing as mind, there is also no such thing as buddha-mind. The self-nature realized after eliminating illusion is also illusory, so it is a mistake to practice with the idea of replacing illusory mind with buddha-mind.

Does this mean you will spend the rest of your life replacing one illusion with another? The *Heart Sutra* says:

> Form is not other than emptiness,
> And emptiness is not other than form.

Form is precisely emptiness,
And emptiness is precisely form.

When form disappears, there is no emptiness to speak of. When the illusory mind disappears, true nature disappears as well. When the illusory mind does not move, true mind is not there. Aspiring to enlightenment makes us diligent, but we should not have that idea in mind when we practice. Even if we became enlightened, we should not think that we have attained anything.

Before practice, people are not aware of their illusory mind; they think that everything they experience is real. After they begin to practice they learn that the mind is illusory. When they finally experience enlightenment, they may think they have replaced illusory mind with true mind. The *Song of Mind* negates this idea: if the nature of mind is non-arising, then neither illusory mind nor true mind exists. Chan Master Linji (d. 867) said that the mind that seeks buddhahood is the mind of samsara. You have come to practice; that is enough. Do not seek anything beyond that.

What need is there of knowledge and views? means that one should not crave knowledge. You may think practice is difficult, but it is actually easy. Just put down your knowledge and views—the sources of vexation—and the mind of illusion will disappear. Scattered mind is only the visible tip of the iceberg; the hidden part is all the knowledge and views that you have accumulated since birth. The way to begin practicing is to first calm your scattered mind.

1.2 ■ Like Waking from a Dream

Originally there is not a single dharma;
Why discuss inspiration and training?

One retreatant here has two problems: he wants to grab hold of something but cannot, and he wants to get rid of his ego but cannot. In fighting himself, he is making more trouble for himself; in trying to eliminate ego, he is making it more tenacious. He is not alone. Everyone has problems with practice. After all, if you had no problems you would already be enlightened.

Niutou says, *Originally there is not a single dharma; why discuss inspiration and training?* Here, "dharma" represents all phenomena, including the Buddhadharma (the teachings of Buddhism). These words may be disturbing to someone seeking remedies for problems that arise in practice. After all, if there are neither dharmas nor Buddhadharma, what guides your practice? Even long-time Chan practitioners wonder what use it all is. This is the wrong attitude. Do not worry whether practice is useless; just focus on the practice itself with no other thought, especially that of enlightenment. Practice is like a dream in which you may walk slow or fast, go near or far, but when you awaken you realize it never really happened. How fast or far you walk in your dream has nothing to do with waking up. One does not practice to become enlightened, but when it happens it is like waking from a dream.

Practice Is Life Itself

> Coming and going without beginning;
> Sought for, it is not seen.

You can tie a piece of meat on the end of a stick and then tie the stick to a dog's back so that meat dangles in front of its face. No matter how much the dog chases the meat, he won't get it. Seeking results in meditation is like this. Here is another analogy: wherever you walk, your shadow follows, so why get disgusted when you can't get rid of it? Trying to get rid of vexations is the same. One more analogy: pet hamsters often have treadmills to keep them occupied. The faster the animal runs, the faster the treadmill turns; but the hamster never gets out of its cage, and the wheel doesn't go anywhere. That is where your practice is going with an anxious, expectant mind—nowhere. The same analogy applies to trying to escape from death and vexation. Who is it that wants to escape? It is the ego, but how can the ego escape vexation if the ego *is* vexation?

One person in the east looks westward and calls it west; another in the west looking eastward calls it east. They are looking at the same thing—it is relative; there is no ultimate east or west. If you run to the west to find its origin, you will be running forever. Trying to pinpoint enlightenment is like trying to find the origin of west or east. *You* want to get enlightened; *you* want to see your true nature; *you* want to be rid of vexation. How is it possible for *you* to get enlightened if it is *you* who can't let go?

Some people hope for blessings or power to practice from a bodhisattva, or the Buddha. Others wish to practice so they can use what they learn to help others. There are still others—and this is the best approach—who see practice as just their entire life. Outside of cultivation there is nothing—life itself becomes practice. They do not try to do anything, yet everything gets done; and when asked, will say they have done nothing. We should aspire to be this type of practitioner. This is what Niutou is talking about.

Some practice to gain something; others resolve to manifest bodhi (awakened) mind, become bodhisattvas, and help sentient beings. Niutou wants us to go one step further and practice without seeking anything.

What Is True Liberation?

> No need to do anything;
> It is bright, still, self-apparent.

From sentient beings' point of view, the Buddha exists, but the Buddha has no conception of being a buddha. If the Buddha thought that he was helping sentient beings, he wouldn't be a buddha. As Master Linji said, trying to become an enlightened patriarch is samsaric karma—a product of the ego.

People who have gotten something from practice often tell me, "Thanks for giving me so much. I've gotten so much benefit." Yet it is my hope that by practicing, you get rid of everything you have, and go away with nothing. The more you obtain, the more trouble it will be for you. If you take home all that has been said, and all that you have been through here, you will take home a lot of trouble. It is useful to listen to what I say at this time, but it is meant for this time; there is no need to keep on thinking about it, or to cling to it.

When you meditate, begin by isolating yourself. First, isolate from your daily life and your daily concerns. Second, isolate from the people and things around you. Third, isolate yourself from your previous and future thoughts and stay in the present moment. There is nothing else to do, because if you are not bothering with your next thought, then you are not chasing after anything.

There is a story about an old Chan monk who was dying. Because his virtue and merit were so great, all the heavenly realms were open to him. He could have encountered bodhisattvas and buddhas, but he realized that if he went to heaven, it would just be a self that goes. He thus decided that there was no place to go or not go.

Just then a demon from hell appeared and said, "I have orders from the king of hell to take you with me."

The old monk said, "I'm not here, so go ahead and take me if you want."

True liberation does not come from wanting to be liberated; in true liberation there is nothing to want, nothing to discard, no place to go, and no place to avoid. It means not being moved by the environment, not having likes and dislikes.

1.3 ▓ Clinging to the Past

> The past is like empty space;
> Know anything and the basic principle
>   is lost.

Without the accumulation of experience, knowledge, and views, there would be no illusory mind. If you never learned the name you were given at birth, you would not know your name today. If you cut yourself off from the past, you won't have any illusory thoughts. In fact, you won't have any thoughts at all, since there are no illusory thoughts in the present moment. Thoughts arise because of attachment to the past and anticipation of the future. We connect these thoughts to make comparisons and judgments. I'm sure all of you were thinking today while sitting on your cushions. Some of your thoughts were of the future, your job, plans, families, friends, and so on. All of these thoughts come from the past. If I scold you for thinking, you might be sad, angry, or happy. Let's say you were happy. This happiness also comes from past experience. You know what to expect from me, and my guidance makes you happy.

The *Song of Mind* says the past is like empty space. Your previous thought is no longer present; neither is the thought before that one, and on and on. There is nothing in the past, which is already gone. Wouldn't it be interesting if the past continued to exist? If a car went down a street and the past continued, then instead of going from one point to another the car would form a continuous entity and block the street. How could we do fast-walking meditation if the past existed? However, even though the past does not exist, we can't seem to stop thinking about it. There is nothing substantial about our past fortunes, misfortunes, successes, and failures; yet, we cling to them.

The argument you had the other day is gone, a thing of the past. Why dwell on it? If we can grasp the principle that the past is like empty space, then one second of practice is all we would need to succeed. There would be no illusory thoughts to deter us.

Today someone said to me, "If the unmoving mind is buddha-nature, I'll just tell my mind not to move." Unfortunately, when you tell your mind not to move, you are moving it. If you say that your mind isn't moving, who is thinking that thought? The mind that feels or thinks these things is moving. It is difficult to have an unmoving mind because we carry so much of our past with us. We may intellectually agree that the past is illusory, yet we hold dearly to it. We are not wholly convinced that our past, our thoughts, and our mind are illusory. That is why we use a practice method—as an illusion to replace our other illusions.

A line of the *Diamond Sutra* reads: "There should not be anywhere that the mind abides." In other words, the mind should not stick to anything. This is wisdom. The second line of verse above says, *Know anything and the basic principle is lost*. If the mind abides on anything, that would be illusion, attachment, and vexation. Thoughts of money, work, or loved ones are vexation, but so are thoughts of enlightenment, wisdom, or buddhahood.

Someone approached me about attending a retreat. She said, "I'm very old. I don't know how much time I have left, so I'm anxious about getting enlightened."

I asked her if she knew how to meditate.

She said, "Yes, but I want to find a master who can help me get enlightened."

I replied, "When people come here I tell them not to think about getting enlightened. Do you still want to come?"

She answered, "If there's no enlightenment here, then I won't attend the retreat. But that's impossible. You say in your books that there is such a thing as enlightenment."

"That's right, but I don't tell people to get enlightened."

The woman thought my words were strange, but they are not strange at all. If you seek after something, that itself is vexation. Seeking enlightenment is vexation. Wherever there is attachment, there also is vexation.

If you were to fall in the ocean, of course you would want to hang onto something to survive. Think about this: all around you is a vast ocean, but you don't want it. You are desperately looking for something to hang onto. As long as there is an ego or self that you hold onto, you cannot be liberated. If you let go of your ego, that is liberation. If you had fallen from the boat and instead thought, "Great. I'm now free from that little boat," you would not be seeking to grasp anything. On the other hand, you may fall into the ocean and think, "I'm dead." That is not liberation; that is death. Someone is truly liberated only if they have no attachments. When there is no attachment, there is no aversion and no fear.

What Is in the Enlightened Mind?

> Casting a clear light on the world,
> Illuminating, yet obscured.

The previous lines say the mind does not exist in time or space. These lines say that the enlightened mind does function, yet there is nothing real or substantial in it that one can point to. An enlightened person still has the will or vow to help sentient beings. Sentient beings perceive a mind to be present, but the enlightened person does not. The mind functions—that is all.

Someone during a lecture asked if enlightened people got angry.

"Yes," I replied.

"That's strange. They shouldn't have any vexation."

I said, "Ordinary people get angry from within, but enlightened people get angry because other people cause them to do so."

The person asked, "How can others make them angry? Their minds should be unmoving, not be affected by others."

"Enlightened people simply reflect things," I answered. "If others are present, then enlightened people will reflect their presence, but there is nothing in them."

When ordinary people get angry, they don't forget. But enlightened people forget their anger the moment that the cause disappears. There is nothing left in them. After a thunderstorm, the sun comes out and everything is beautiful again. The thunder and rain are gone. All that is left is the beautiful day. If, after the weather cleared, it continued to rain and thunder, that would be strange.

There is a priest in Taiwan who is the president of a university. One of his students said that this priest gets angry, but afterward, it is as if nothing happened. Perhaps because he is a cleric, he only argues for other people's sake. Since it has nothing to do with him, why should the anger linger? Cultivating this skill would be good, but it is difficult because of our attachments. When we fight with our loved ones, it is hard to forget because they are part of us. If someone takes your money, you cannot forget because you think the money belongs to you.

If the mind does not exist in time and space, then there is nothing in the mind. Whatever happens in the mind can be put down so that nothing remains. It's now halfway through the retreat. Do you still have things you cannot put down? You may say, "I am meditating well, and I feel good. I guess it's all right if I think about other things for a while." Then things change; you're not counting your breaths well and you think, "I'm doing poorly now." These thoughts arise because your mind clings to the past and thinks about good and bad.

I have been talking about throwing away the past, but you should throw away the present as well. Realize, however, that throwing away the past and present doesn't mean having a blank mind. You are still aware of things, yet the mind is clear and unattached.

1.4 ※ One-Mind Is Still Attached to Self

> If one-mindedness is impeded,
> All dharmas are misunderstood.

You came to this retreat in hopes of improving your practice and clearing your minds through meditation. If you had greater expectations, perhaps I discouraged you when I said that meditating has nothing to do with becoming enlightened. One of you wondered what the point of meditating is, if it does not lead to enlightenment. The answer is that while meditation does not lead to enlightenment, if you do not meditate you will never be enlightened. It is true that some rare people can get enlightened without practicing. This is called "liberation through wisdom." Shakyamuni Buddha's first disciples became liberated when they heard him expound the Four Noble Truths. The scriptures speak of people getting enlightened after hearing a few words from the Buddha.

While getting enlightened does not depend on meditation, sitting is still useful for calming the mind. This is because our minds are usually so scattered that enlightenment is impossible. What if your mind is not scattered? What if, as one of you told me, you sometimes don't have any thoughts? Your awareness of having no thoughts is itself a thought. At the very least, you still have a concept of self. I venture that you have thoughts even when you think you have none, except that you are unaware of them. The Buddha said that in the mind of the ordinary person, no less than sixty-four thoughts come and go every *ksana*, a fraction of a second. These thoughts arise because we are influenced by the three poisons (*klesas*) of desire, aversion, and ignorance. Because of them, our minds cannot help but constantly move. Only by transcending the three poisons can the mind stop moving.

Now I will say something that may seem like a contradiction to my previous words, but in fact, agrees with Niutou. Even if your mind stops for an instant—regardless of what it stops on—that is still an obstruction, and you have lost direction. In this condition, no dharmas can be understood. A mind that stops on something, whether internal or external, is not an unmoving mind because it is attached to that something. The mind will always be attached either to an object, or to the self. Either case presupposes that a self is present. But as long as a self is present, dharmas cannot be understood.

When the mind stops on external phenomena and internal wandering thoughts, it is still scattered. There is "I," "you," and "it," a subject and its environment. Amidst these diverse phenomena, a self must be present. But even when there is no object for the mind to stop on, when there is no environment and nothing relative to the self (as in deep samadhi, or meditative absorption), a sense of self still exists. This is also not enlightenment.

If the mind stops on anything, there is no enlightenment. However, practitioners, especially beginners, need to hold on to something to collect the mind. This is why we have a method: an object for the mind to attach to, pulling the mind toward one point. This is still attachment, but it is a necessary requirement in the early stages of practice.

I have often outlined the stages of practice in the following way: we start with a scattered mind and no method. With a method we can eventually work toward a concentrated mind. With diligence and determination, concentration will improve until quite naturally, we evolve to the one-mind state of samadhi. However, in samadhi the mind still stops on one-mind, or the self. We must go beyond one-mind to no-mind. Here the mind truly stops on nothing. Only here can one truly be in accordance with all dharmas.

Unmoving Mind Still Functions

> Coming and going thus,
> Is there need for thorough investigation?

To say that the mind stops at something does not mean that it is not moving. The mind stops because it attaches to things; and the mind attaches to things because it moves. When the mind is unmoving there is no attachment, and nothing on which it stops. Some critics surmise, then, that the unmoving mind is like a corpse, a rock, or a block of wood. This is not the case. A person who truly understands dharmas still "comes and goes." Coming and going may be understood on two levels. First, it may seem that in the enlightened mind, thoughts, feelings, judgments, words, and actions come and go. But these comings and goings are outside one's mind; within, it is still. In effect, at this time there is no mind, only sentient beings and phenomena. They have nothing to do with the enlightened person who still thinks, speaks, and acts spontaneously in response to sentient beings.

Second, indeed there is coming and going, but all within the mind. Since all coming and going is confined to one's mind, in effect there is no coming and going. For instance, if you pass a coin from the left hand to the right and vice versa, the coin has still not left you. All sentient beings are this one self, which is not separate from all sentient beings. Thus, there is no separate mind to speak of. Sentient beings appear to be moving, but the mind is not moving. Since the mind is not moving, and all sentient beings are really this mind, then sentient beings are not moving. If all things are already in one's mind, as Niutou himself asks, why investigate anything?

Still we investigate *huatous* (short questions that point to the nature of ultimate reality) and count breaths to still the mind, and for what purpose? Is it to see buddha-nature? But buddha-nature is always and originally present. We do not perceive it because we have vexations that have always been present. Buddhism refrains from talking about the origins of buddha-nature and sentient beings. What would be the purpose? Buddhism is pragmatic and seeks to clear away vexations so that buddha-nature may manifest. This is easy to accomplish. When the mind disappears, buddha-nature naturally appears, but buddha-nature is present even when the mind is scattered and vexed.

One can compare the mind of vexation and buddha-nature to a wavy, moving line, and a still, straight one. The two lines may appear to be different, but if we pull the ends of the moving line taut and hold it steady, then it becomes straight and still. When the line is constantly moving, it is difficult to see clearly its true nature. We can say that the straight, still line represents buddha-nature, and the moving line represents vexation, but both lines have the same nature, and the deluded mind is not different from buddha-nature.

When the mind stops discriminating, buddha-nature manifests. Even saying this can be misleading, for it makes it seem as if buddha-nature is different from ordinary mind, as if it is hiding until the deluded mind goes away. The deluded mind is already buddha-nature. Therefore, it is pointless to speak about the origin of the deluded mind. It has no beginning because it is not other than buddha-nature. If deluded mind has a beginning then buddha-nature must also have a beginning.

Someone today asked me if all sentient beings' wandering thoughts were joined with one buddha-nature, or if each sentient being had a separate and different buddha-nature. In other words, is buddha-nature different for each sentient being? Is the nature of water in the Pacific different from the nature of water in the Atlantic? Is the nature of wind in the east different from the nature of wind in the west? It is the same water and the same wind.

Buddha-nature is neither divisible nor static. That is why one can say that all sentient beings come and go within the mind of an enlightened being. The enlightened mind may be unmoving, yet it is active. The mind still functions, but more directly and clearly than the deluded mind. In the enlightened mind you will find no attachment or discrimination. Thoughts arise spontaneously in response to others and have nothing to do with the enlightened person. It would be quite meaningless to ask them how many sentient beings they have helped. The only answer would be that sentient beings are helped according to causes and conditions. If causes and conditions are ripe for an individual, then that individual will be helped.

It is said that the Buddha delivers all sentient beings. However, only those whose causes and conditions are ripe for accepting the Buddha-dharma will benefit. Those whose conditions are not ripe cannot be helped; perhaps they do not need help, were helped in the past, or will meet the right conditions in the future. For example, two hundred years ago few people in the West knew of Buddhadharma, and fewer still were willing to accept it. In the last fifty years many Westerners have begun to study and practice the Dharma, and teachers have come to spread it. Causes and conditions for the West and Buddhadharma are ripening. It seems that they will ripen further, for Westerners appear to have a thirst for the Dharma. Whether they study Chan, Zen, Tibetan, or Theravada Buddhism, this is good. People have different affinities, but it is the same Dharma. It is like a good business that supplies what the people need and want. If causes and conditions change, and people lose interest in Buddhism, that is all right too. Change is the nature of things. If later on no one is interested in my teachings, that is fine. I will be out of a job and I will have more time to meditate.

The goal of practice is to have nothing in your mind. Only then will you accord with dharmas. Check to see if you still have attachments in your mind. If you cannot empty your mind of attachments instantly, then you must use a method to lessen them. If you must have paintings on the walls of your mind, at least keep them simple, and try not to have too many. As time goes on, hopefully the pictures will get smaller and fewer, until there is only one picture, that of the self. If you get to that point, we can go to the next step.

1.5 ▪ Spontaneous Wisdom

> Arising without the mark of arising,
> Arising and illumination are the same.

The *Diamond Sutra* says, "With the mind not abiding in anything, the mind arises." People may misinterpret this as saying that there is something called "mind" that arises. Niutou corrects this error by saying that enlightened mind arises, but it is not the arising of ordinary, deluded mind.

Because the true Dharma is ineffable, explaining it leads to trouble. For this reason Chan masters often say cryptic things like: *Arising without the mark of arising.* Hearing or reading this, people may think that if there is no mark of arising then there is no mind. To correct this error Niutou then says: *Arising and illumination are the same.*

If there is no arising, how can there be illumination? Remember that Niutou is referring to the enlightened mind. What arises in the enlightened mind is wisdom that spontaneously responds to sentient beings. Because "mind" is ordinarily associated with a "self" that goes with it, we call this natural response "illumination," the enlightened state.

Question: If there are no sentient beings to receive illumination, does it still exist?

Sheng Yen: When there are no sentient beings, there is no illumination to speak of. Illumination only exists in relation to others. The needs of others are met by the illumination of enlightened beings. If there were no sentient beings, there would be no need for the Buddha's wisdom. If something is not used, its function is not evident. If you don't light a match, its function—to make a flame—is not seen. If no one ever looks at a painting, is it a painting? No. It is just an object.

Student: In other words, nothing has intrinsic value other than through its interaction with other sentient beings. So, if we take a painting, the only interaction it can have is that people can look at it and treat it as a painting. If no one looks at it, the object does not exist as a painting.

Sheng Yen: Previously I talked about wavy and straight lines. A wavy line represents vexation, a straight one buddha-nature. If you pull the ends of a wavy line taut, it becomes straight. The two lines have the same potential of being either wavy or straight. If a mind has no vexations, then it is the same as buddha-nature. Today, someone in an interview asked, "In that case, if I sit and attain one-mind, my mind doesn't move. Isn't that the same as the straight line? Doesn't that mean that one-mind is the same as no-mind?"

This is a grave error and again points out the danger of relying on intellect and language. A mind of vexation is a mind in motion, and I compared it to a wavy line. If there are no vexations, then there is no-mind. But to make the analogy fit perfectly, one should say that with no-mind, the line disappears.

One-mind is different from no-mind. First, there are many levels of one-mindedness, but even at the highest level, there is still a self. If we were to use the analogy of the line, one-mind would appear to be straight, but on closer analysis one would discover minute and subtle waves in it. One-mind still has vexations and attachments.

Question: So does "no-mind" mean mind without a self?

Sheng Yen: To avoid confusion, one should not even call a mind without a self a "mind." One should call it "wisdom," or "illumination."

Student: What does "mind" mean, then?

Sheng Yen: That depends on the context. The ordinary mind is illusory and deluded. However, in the title *Song of Mind*, "mind" refers to true mind, or no-mind. Mind without a self, therefore, can still be called a mind, but in fact it is no-mind, or wisdom. Niutou urges us to transcend deluded mind and realize true mind.

All these questions are useless, especially on a Chan retreat. If you try to find your way by theoretical, philosophical reasoning, you will get nowhere. You may as well go home and curl up with a good book. It is just more fodder for the deluded mind. I hope my words help your practice, but if you rely on theoretical understanding, then you are on the wrong track.

Practicing without Goals

> Desiring to purify the mind,
> There is no mind for effort.

People here spend the day practicing, trying to purify their minds, yet somehow it does not seem to work. Some of you say, "I tell my mind to shut up, but it keeps on talking." Others say, "I get more and more discouraged. I have no confidence at this point. I have no control over my mind." Others don't even know how to breathe. Still others cannot even control their bodies, let alone their minds. Is it necessary to go to the bathroom after every sitting? I doubt that all of you have bladder problems.

All these problems begin with the mind not settling down. If you calm your mind and use it to practice, pains or itches won't distract you, and you won't have to urinate all the time. You will not look for diversions; practice alone is sufficient. Some of you have sat well and do not feel like stirring. You do not want anything to disturb your practice. This is using your mind to practice. Sitting well is good and you can derive great benefit from it, but it is not enough. It is still not Chan. Using your mind to practice still involves the self. You still have attachments. For one thing, you enjoy the peaceful feeling and want it to continue. Self-centeredness is present. Niutou says one must *purify the mind*, which means to have no attachments, no desire, and no self-centeredness. If you are working hard with an aim to purify your mind, you will only add more problems. That is not to say that you should not work hard, but that you should not work with a goal in mind. Furthermore, if you do succeed in purifying the mind, that mind will continue to work hard, but with no attachment.

There is only one day left, so practice for the sake of practice, not for wisdom or anything else. Do not seek to lose vexation and attachments; instead, put your mind on the practice method. Do not fight or oppose wandering thoughts, just ignore them. If you feel drowsy or lazy, exert yourself and put energy into the practice. Often, people spend half their time fighting wandering thoughts. They get tired, become drowsy, and daydream. When they regain their energy, they resume the struggle. They spend the entire retreat battling and sleeping, battling and sleeping.

If you are anxious about getting results, you will expend too much energy and become tired. On the other hand, if you are lax you will not be successful either. Your practice should be like a fine stream that flows constantly. It should not be like a volcano, dormant one moment, exploding the next. A good practitioner uses minimal energy, but maintains this energy continuously and uninterruptedly, staying on the method.

Throughout time and space nothing is illuminated

2.1 ■ Cultivating Nonattachment

> Throughout time and space nothing is
> illuminated;
> This is most profound.

When we start to practice we can talk about space and time, but when we reach the other shore of wisdom, neither space nor time matters. During retreat you should progressively isolate yourself, first, from the outside world; second, from people and situations; and third, from the previous and succeeding thoughts. In other words, keep your mind in the present moment. This way, your sense of space and time will gradually diminish until mind alone exists. With such an attitude, you will surely be successful in practice.

Attachments to time and space create vexations, but if you are fully engaged in practice, time and space are no longer problems. After enlightenment time and space still exist, but there is no attachment to them. You can help sentient beings without the idea that you are doing so. To be unattached to space and time is thus a profound attainment. Only with no attachments can one truly help others. Isolating yourself on retreat is the way to begin to cultivate such nonattachment.

I have told you time and again not to seek enlightenment, but for some the idea is too seductive. Your imagination hooks you, and you practice with this intent. But as you try to rid your life of vexations, you get more. As you reach for enlightenment, it eludes you.

When you practice, it is best not to have any attachments at all, but this is impossible for ordinary sentient beings. You have to begin by separating yourself from the external environment. Narrow the environment to yourself, and then drop that as well. While this is quite difficult, it is still not the ultimate goal of practice. Ultimately time, space, and self must again exist. Without self, nothing exists, and if nothing exists, it is impossible to help others. Ultimate liberation is when time, space, and self exist, but not for you. At this stage you can help others without attachment.

In the first stage of practice, time, space, yourself, and sentient beings exist in your mind. In the second stage, time, space, yourself, and sentient beings no longer exist. In stage three you actively engage time, space, and others, but are no longer attached to them. Some students become frustrated after practicing a short time without getting enlightened. Maybe it's my guidance. People come here thinking they have a chance to become enlightened, and I tell them to forget about it. If you want only the luscious ripe apple at the topmost branch, you will likely go home empty-handed.

Do not pay attention to your body and mind while you practice. If you pay too much attention to your body, you'll be distracted by discomfort. If you pay too much attention to your mind, you'll be disappointed when you cannot control it. Mind and body are always connected. When you feel sleepy, you may scold yourself for being lazy, but it may actually be that your body needs rest. Also, if you have a scattered mind, your body contributes to it. However, if you practice in the present moment, your mind will become concentrated, and your awareness of space, time, and self will lessen.

If you are very sleepy, then you must sleep a while. Pain is a different story. I guarantee that pain will not kill or injure you. Unless you know that you have serious physical problems, I suggest that you ignore the pain. If you can't ignore it, then endure it. Watch pain with an objective mind and it will transform into coolness. If you detach from the previous thought and stay in the present moment, you will not see, hear, or feel anything. You won't even feel that you exist, let alone the pain in your legs. If you don't exist, how can pain?

2.2 ▦ The True Knowing Is Not Knowing

> Knowing dharmas is non-knowing;
> Non-knowing is knowing the essential.

Chan does not rely on language. Therefore, if you understand Buddha-dharma only with your intellect, then you do not understand it at all. Some people study a *gong'an* (an anecdote that points to the nature of ultimate reality) or a *huatou* and try to solve it intellectually, but any competent Chan master will detect any trace of intellect in the answer. You can intellectually understand the concepts and principles of Buddha-dharma, but that is only one type of understanding. Enlightenment does not come from mere intellectual knowledge. As far as enlightenment is concerned, to think that you know is, in fact, ignorance. Those who have studied the sutras (Buddhist scriptures) may think that they know Buddhadharma, but it is like looking at the world through a telescope; what you see is limited, what you understand is partial.

The essence of Buddhism is wisdom and compassion, so Buddhists know they should be compassionate, but inevitably someone or something irritates them, and they lose sight of this teaching. In ordinary people wisdom is shallow and limited, and to be compassionate all the time is impossible. I know a monk who is outwardly nice to everyone, but who confessed to me that since he can't show his anger, he finds release in privately cutting up his clothes and books. This isn't too bad. At least he doesn't beat himself. Still, his wisdom and compassion are not deep.

We are human, so we get angry. To cope better, when you feel angry, relax your abdomen and then tell yourself, "Okay, now you can be angry." It's more difficult to be angry once you are relaxed. The abdomen tightens when one is angry.

A prerequisite to progress on the path is to realize that you are ignorant. The more you think you know, the more vexations you have. Knowing the details but not the underlying principles, you get lost in a sea of facts.

A Brahman in Shakyamuni Buddha's time thought he knew everything and wanted to debate the Buddha. First, he tied his head and stomach with copper bands. When Shakyamuni asked what the bands were for, he said, "I have so much knowledge I must bind my head and stomach so they don't explode." Then he challenged the Buddha, "If you ask a question I cannot answer, I'll be your disciple. If you lose, then you'll be my disciple."

The Buddha said, "I have no questions to ask."

The Brahman said, "How can we debate if you have no topic?"

The Buddha replied, "As long as something can be debated, it can be refuted by clever argument. But since I have nothing to debate, you cannot defeat me. You, on the other hand, have so many ideas, it will be easy to defeat you."

Those who have no understanding of Buddhadharma should study its concepts and principles. However, those who have only an intellectual understanding of Buddhadharma are also encouraged to practice. For those who have been successful on the path, there is no such thing as Buddhadharma. They might speak about it, but it is only in response to those who don't know about it.

Confucius once encountered a notorious bandit who had nine thousand followers. Confucius tried to reform the outlaw through reasoning, but no matter what Confucius said, the bandit rejected the attempts to reform him. The point of the story is that "silence is better than words." Even Confucius had his limitations. In the end, it's better if there are no words.

You should nurture faith as you practice the Buddhadharma. Try not to analyze everything or endlessly speculate. Refrain from asking so many questions; just practice. Whatever you understand with knowledge is not genuine understanding. When I practiced Zen in Japan, I had already received my doctorate. My *roshi* (Zen master) knew this and took particular delight in scolding me.

People who like to read Buddhist literature usually try to find connections between the words and their own experiences. Some people turn to books for guidance instead of finding a qualified teacher. They'll remain ignorant. This explains Niutou's statement, *Knowing dharmas is non-knowing.*

Non-knowing is knowing the essential reminds me of a story about a boss who needed an assistant. Ten people applied for the job and they all did well on the written test. At the interviews, all but one boasted of what they knew, but the last one said he didn't know anything. He said he was willing to learn, to ask questions, and to check with the boss if he had any difficulty. He was the one who was hired. In the same way, it is best that you come to a retreat without previous knowledge. Begin as if you had no past. Those who think they know everything cannot move forward. On the other hand, those who have tremendous wisdom sometimes appear stupid. If your stomach were infinitely large, there would be no need to eat because nothing would be outside your stomach.

True knowing is not knowing. One truly knows only when one has true wisdom. Knowledge is limited, while wisdom is boundless. A woman called from California and said she wanted to come to one of my retreats. She said she had read my books, and they were in accordance with what she knew. This person, who thinks she knows, doesn't know. If she thinks she doesn't know, but has the mind to learn, then she has the correct mind for practice. The greatest error is to look at Buddhadharma with eyes full of past experiences and knowledge.

Not knowing, one can begin to know. A blank sheet of paper can be used, but if it is already filled with scribbles it is not of much use. Be like a blank sheet of paper. To do this, cut yourself off from the previous thought and stay with the present one.

A participant on this retreat subconsciously seeks something to clear herself like a white marker board. There are traces of previous writings on the marker board, just as there are lingering thoughts in even the clearest of minds. To become like the clear white board, one must be diligent and thorough in one's practice.

When a thought comes up, just say, "I don't know you. I don't recognize you." When working on a *gong'an* or *huatou*, you must not think or speculate. One participant came to me after only two hours of working on a *huatou*, and told me he now knew that *wu* was buddha-nature. I asked how he came to that realization, and he said that the Buddha's teaching says so. However, he was perplexed because he didn't feel changed. I told him that any enlightenment that could come so easily and in such a manner could only be a joke. I told him to reserve such answers for written exams, not Chan retreats.

When practicing in the non-knowing state, you will not know what you are eating or where you are walking, but you will feel comfortable and light. There will be power in your practice. At this point you can truly work on a *huatou*. If you can approach it with this mindset, the great doubt will arise quickly, and you will benefit. But if your head is loaded with knowledge and experience, then practicing a *gong'an* or *huatou* is a waste of time. My Zen master had good reason to scold me. My mind was loaded with too much knowledge.

2.3 ▪ Levels of Quietude

> Using the mind to maintain quietude,
> You still fail to leave the sickness.

These two lines offer an important caution for serious practitioners: meditation can result in Chan sickness. One participant here has been in a pleasant dream state for three days, yet she thinks her mind is clear. This is an illusory state, a sickness, in fact. On the surface her mind appears to be calm, but it is moving. She's not working hard; she might as well be on vacation, or asleep. It is a pleasant experience for a beginning practitioner, but an obstacle for a person intent on entering samadhi or dhyana. In fact, she may become attached to this experience and habitually try to recapture it. If she does this, she will find it difficult to make progress.

On one retreat someone constantly cracked his knuckles. I asked why he did this, and he said it was because there was nothing else to do. His actions and words revealed a scattered, undisciplined mind. He was bored. I also hear people cracking their knuckles on this retreat. I see people scratching and stretching and moving. I hear people sighing. It tells me you are bored, as if you had nothing to do. Please train yourself to be mindful and attend to your method.

There are three levels of tranquillity, or quietude. The first is external: an environment free of distractions. The most distracting noises come from people talking, laughing, crying, and moving. These are more disturbing than random noises from the outside. The quietest way to practice is alone, but next best is to be on a retreat where people are quiet. For this reason we do not allow talking during retreats. If people laugh, cry, or move around, you will have to deal with it, but that should not happen too often.

At the second, deeper level of quietude, noises from the environment no longer matter. You are so intently focused on the method that external sounds are not heard, or if heard, they are not a problem. The mind is still moving, but it is on the method. This is a good level to be at.

The third level of quietude is where the mind does not seem to move. Everything is still. When you start the retreat, you should already have reached the first level of quietude. As you progress, you should be able to reach the second level, where noises do not bother you. By now I'm sure most of you have experienced the second level at least once. Some of you may have reached the third level, and that is good. However, it is not enlightenment; it isn't even samadhi or dhyana.

Do not attach to any level. At the second level of quietude, one might see visions of buddhas, bodhisattvas, or the Pure Land. If one becomes too strongly attached to them, one can enter a demonic state of mind.

Getting stuck at the third level of quietude is called "sitting in a ghost's cave on Black Mountain." Even though it feels liberating, you are cutting off a chance to experience wisdom. Some people even think they have entered nirvana. It's like eating something delicious and becoming addicted to it. Every time you sit you will strive to reach that place of quietude. Reaching it, you will not want to leave; not reaching it, you will be vexed. This can become a serious obstruction.

Using a method like *huatou*, *gong'an*, or silent illumination (*shikantaza* in Zen) helps to keep you from getting stuck in the second or third level of quietude. If one has cultivated the stillness of the third level, then working on a *huatou* or *gong'an* should give rise to the doubt sensation. In turn, the doubt sensation will turn into a great mass of doubt. Finally, when the mass of doubt dissolves, one will see into one's own nature.

Gong'an and *huatou* are active methods that break through and go beyond quietude. It would be wrong to say that what lies beyond is tranquillity, but it would also be wrong to say it is not tranquillity. What lies beyond is the realm of Chan.

On the other hand, silent illumination is not as forceful a method as gong'an or *huatou*. "Silence" means that the mind is not attached to anything. "Illumination" means that the mind clearly perceives all that is going on—sights, sounds, as well as its own conditions. This illumination is different from pure tranquillity in that the illuminated mind is perceptive and aware of everything that is happening.

This silent awareness is not limited to sitting meditation; it can happen when you are prostrating, during walking meditation, or in daily living. When you prostrate, you can reach a level where the body is moving on its own and the mind is calm. With walking meditation you can get to the point where the mind is clear, and the body moves on its own. This is not purely tranquil. Chan uses both tranquillity and activity. Making use of both tranquillity and awareness is like using both feet to move forward, rather than hopping on one.

2.4 ▪ Experience the Great Death

> Birth and death forgotten—
> This is original nature.

These two lines are especially important for Chan practitioners. One participant told me that he plans to stay at the Chan Center indefinitely. I said, "In that case, on this retreat you must be determined to let your body turn to ash. Put any concerns about birth and death out of your mind." Someone came to retreat with many worries. I told her to simply put them aside because there was nothing to worry about. I told another who complained of leg pains that the more it hurts, the better. Someone else feels great heat in her body and another person has stomach problems.

Everyone's situation is different and demands individual adjustment and guidance. Heed the judgment of the retreat master. If I tell you not to worry about a particular pain, then don't worry about it. On the other hand, if I tell you not to push too hard, then take it easier.

Legend has it that when Shakyamuni Buddha sat for six years, wheat grew through his skin and bones. His six years of intensive sitting did not damage his legs. After attaining complete enlightenment, he was able to walk around India for nearly fifty years, spreading Buddhadharma. Don't be so concerned with the pain in your legs that you must pamper them with balms and oils. Put your mind on the practice.

On a Chan retreat, be prepared to go through a "great death." While you are alive, make use of your body and practice diligently. Do not concern yourself with matters of life and death. Who knows when death will come?

Someone said to me, "Once I die I can no longer practice. I haven't reached enlightenment yet, so isn't it wise to take care of my body so that I can make good use of it while I practice?" This is a wrong attitude. He is holding on too much to the importance of the body. Buddhadharma speaks of five perverted views, of which the most harmful is attaching to one's body. This is the most difficult obstacle in practice.

For most people, birth and death refer to the physical body, but an advanced practitioner also understands that each thought also undergoes birth and death; every second, thoughts arise and perish. Those who fully understand this do not fear and do not cling to their ideas. But I doubt any of us are at that point yet. We think of death in terms of our physical bodies, and we fear it. We don't know what comes next, and no explanation fully convinces or comforts us. Those who fear death do not have deep conviction in Buddhadharma, which says that though the body dies, life and death go on continuously.

Some older people approach me about attending retreats, and want to be assured that they will be enlightened if they attend. It seems that if they have no assurance that they will reach buddhahood before dying, they are reluctant to put in the effort. This is a bad attitude.

We practice for the sake of practice, not to get enlightened. If we die before we get enlightened, having practiced is still good, and makes a difference. The opposite attitude is also bad—that there will be future opportunities to practice, so there is no urgency now. Some would rather have a good time in this life and begin to work hard next time around, but they have no idea what conditions will await them. We are fortunate to encounter Buddhadharma in this life, so we should use our good karma to secure our relationship with the Dharma. That way there will be no fear that in our next life we will miss hearing the Dharma. If you let the opportunity slip away, what guarantee do you have that you will meet similar conditions in your next life?

There is a saying in Buddhism: to be fortunate enough to be born a human, and to encounter Buddhadharma, is as rare as a turtle pushing its head through a hole in a piece of flotsam at sea. If we have such rare and fortunate karma, we ought to make good use of the opportunity. Whether or not we get enlightened in this life should not be a concern. There is nothing to be happy about in being alive, and there is nothing fearful in dying. But while we are alive we should make good use of our bodies and minds.

Buddhadharma speaks of two kinds of birth and death. The first is the "sectional-birth-and-death" of each physical lifetime. The second is the "transformational-birth-and-death," of wisdom and merit that simultaneously arise with the death of ignorance and vexation. Bodhisattvas experience transformational-birth-and-death as they make progress toward full enlightenment. As practitioners, our pains are part of our experience of sectional-birth-and-death. When you can put aside concern for the body, you can truly make progress. Eventually you will completely resolve the problem of sectional-birth-and-death and attain transformational-birth-and-death. You will see your original nature and give birth to sagehood.

The greater your attachment to life, the greater will be your fear of death. This will bind you to the cycle of birth indefinitely. But if you can transcend the problem of birth and death, you will leave behind samsara, and attain transformational-birth-and-death.

Since all dharmas are created by the mind, what you think about and cling to will influence what kind of rebirth you will have. Therefore, your attitude or disposition is extremely important. If you do things single-mindedly, but have a negative disposition, it will most likely lead to bad consequences. On the other hand, if you practice for the sake of practice, then most likely you will encounter Buddhadharma in your next life, and practice will come easily and naturally.

There are three important conditions for success in practice. The first is to have faith in Buddhadharma and faith in oneself; the second is to practice diligently; the third is to be determined. Drop your concern for birth and death; for the sake of practice, be willing to let your body and bones go to ashes.

I add a fourth condition, and that is to make a great vow. To make a great vow is to say, "Even though I cannot presently forget birth and death, I vow to eventually do so, and I will allow the power of this great vow to continuously push me forward to that end."

Every time you sit, make a vow not to concern yourself with problems of the body, and of birth and death. Not that you want to die, but that you want to let go of attachment to the body. Don't be rigid and aggressive, but keep a relaxed body and mind. When the mind is relaxed, it is stable, and practice is smooth. When you are nervous, you just create more vexation.

If you have no concern for birth and death, then you also have no concern for time. Don't be anxious for the bell to end a sitting period. Don't think about how well or how poorly you are meditating. Just attend to your practice method.

2.5 ▪ Enlightened Mind Is Not Bound, Not Free

> The highest principle cannot be explained;
> It is neither free nor bound.

These lines say that the Buddhadharma, the highest principle, cannot be explained with words and concepts. When you energetically work on a *huatou*, when you no longer feel pain from sitting, when you react spontaneously to an experience, these are examples of what can result from intensive practice. These are useful experiences, and can lay the foundation for practice. Having them will make it difficult to give up practicing. Without them, people would only remember the pain and might give up. They can be useful while seeking the highest principle, but they are not signs of enlightenment. These phenomena can be explained, but the highest principle, enlightenment, cannot. When you attain the highest principle you will realize that nothing has happened. Actually, things do change and happen, but it is useless to speak of them. When you experience enlightenment, you will understand this.

Conventionally, we speak of being bound by vexation, and then being freed by realizing the highest principle. But *It is neither free nor bound* says that the enlightened mind feels neither bound nor free. Many people feel blissful at the end of retreat. You may feel relaxed and peaceful. This is because your mind is light. It's good, but it is not enlightenment. A Buddhist term for this feeling can be translated as "light and peaceful." Light means that you feel physically weightless and burden-free, peaceful that you enjoy dreamless sleep. These are elementary benefits of being light and peaceful. However, if you do not continue to practice, you will regress. Your body will again feel heavy and dreams will return.

> Lively and attuned to everything,
> It is always right before you.

The highest Buddhadharma cannot be explained; nor does it need to be. People at this level are neither free of nor bound by the world, yet are not disconnected from it. They still respond to the needs of others and help spontaneously and naturally. Enlightened beings do not have to reason or deliberate, since wisdom and compassion naturally arise within them.

Such people do not make plans, yet they are constantly busy. Bodhisattvas help sentient beings and sentient beings help bodhisattvas. Without sentient beings, there would be no reason for bodhisattvas to practice. In Shakyamuni Buddha's time, a jealous disciple named Devadatta vowed in a past life to create obstacles for the Buddha over countless lifetimes. But by doing this, he unwittingly helped Shakyamuni attain buddhahood. The karmic consequences of Devadatta's actions landed him in the hellish realms, but he did not suffer. In fact, legend says that Devadatta sits happily in hell and comments that people in the heavens are not as happy as he is. Devadatta was not afraid of suffering. He was in fact practicing the bodhisattva path. The *Lotus Sutra* says that Devadatta will ultimately achieve buddhahood.

Some practitioners may have the goal of attaining buddhahood or at least liberation from samsara, but Chan practitioners should not. Chan practitioners cultivate the path for the sake of sentient beings. After buddhahood there are no longer sentient beings to help, yet helping still occurs. At all times, Chan practitioners should regard themselves lightly and not put too much importance on their own actions.

If you cannot let go of the self, you will always be bound by your attachment, no matter how hard you practice. Liberation will elude you. If you can lessen your attachment and selfishness, and just practice, then even if you do not attain enlightenment, you will at least have far fewer vexations.

There is nothing in front of you

3.1 ■ For Now, Only the Method Exists

> There is nothing in front of you;
> Nothing, yet everything is as usual.

Attaching to experiences will disturb your practice, and minding your surroundings will put you off the method. To immerse yourself in the method, you must therefore see and hear nothing. As Niutou says, *There is nothing in front of you*.

Today as I walked by someone who was drifting and dozing, he snapped to attention. I'm sure he realized he was not practicing well and started over with renewed effort. If his mind was concentrated, he would not have noticed me, or if he did, would have paid no attention. This isn't miraculous; in daily life, when you are deeply engrossed in a book or conversation, you are oblivious to everything else. You can do the same with your practice.

A scattered mind is diverted by the slightest disturbances. At the beginning of a retreat, I ask people to isolate themselves from the environment. If you did this wholeheartedly, you would not even hear someone whispering in your ear. Disturbances also come from within your mind. Therefore, I also ask you to isolate yourself from thoughts of the past, which no longer exists, and from the future, which does not yet exist. Most importantly, for now, only the method exists.

Some of you have told me that noises do not disturb your practice. You are fully aware of your surroundings, yet unmoved by it. This is good. It is also a good sign when one gets to the point where the method disappears, and there is only silence and clarity. Practitioners of *shikantaza* and silent illumination are familiar with this.

When one starts practicing, the mind is scattered and disturbed by the environment. Once concentration is achieved, you should no longer perceive sights and sounds. When the mind is so settled that the method disappears, you perceive the environment again but without attachment or judgment. However, this is not yet enlightenment, just unified mind.

In the enlightened state that is beyond unified mind, everything is again normal—things are just as they are. Your spouse is still your spouse; fire is hot and ice is cold. However, you do not attach to your discriminations.

Here is a true story. A practitioner at another temple thought he had attained a high level of attainment. He put some excrement on his plate and sat at the table ready to eat with everyone else. He was trying to make a point that to him excrement and food were all the same—that he was beyond discrimination. The master was not in the habit of eating feces and had never heard of the Buddha doing it either, so he asked the practitioner to leave the temple.

Enlightened beings observe normal conventions without being attached or disturbed by them. After his enlightenment the Buddha lived the life of a monk and advised his disciples to do the same. But he still saw Yasodhara as his former wife, and Rahula as his son. Relationships still exist for fully enlightened people, but they do not experience greed, anger, attachment, or other vexations.

There is nothing in front of you is true for the person with a deep practice, as well as for one who has completed the practice. Someone deeply immersed in practice does not perceive the environment, and therefore is not disturbed by it. On the other hand, while clearly perceiving the environment, the enlightened person responds to it without being disturbed.

Isolating oneself is not so much a method as an attitude. Whichever method you use, you can apply the attitude of isolation, but you cannot force yourself not to be disturbed by the environment; it is simply a result of proper practice.

Enlightenment Is Without Attributes

> Do not belabor wisdom to examine it;
> Substance itself is empty and obscure.

People cannot live without a certain amount of understanding and knowledge, so they rely on intellect and experience. Enlightened practitioners rely not on their knowledge or understanding but on wisdom. These lines say that there is no use for knowledge; on the other hand, there is no use for wisdom either. This may sound shocking, but though Niutou wrote the *Song of Mind* with a mind of wisdom, we can only read it with a mind of knowledge. Practitioners need to use their mind of knowledge, but after enlightenment they use wisdom. Knowledge is necessary to understand how to practice, what direction to take, and what goal to work toward. However, in the midst of practice, concerning yourself with knowledge is an obstruction and a waste of time. Also, comparing meditation and practice with your other experiences only creates obstacles. Finally, you cannot possibly imagine when or how you will become enlightened, so it is pointless to speculate. And once enlightened, you will find it impossible to explain it. Using wisdom to explain your experience is also pointless.

A lay practitioner advised his son to practice Chan in order to become enlightened. When the son asked how enlightenment would help him, the father said that it would enable him to know everything. The son said, "I'm having trouble in school. If I get enlightened, will I understand my subjects?" The father told him that he would know everything and would be smarter than Einstein was. Hearing this, the young man decided to work for enlightenment.

Will enlightenment make you omniscient? In fact, enlightenment has nothing to do with knowledge or wisdom. During Shakyamuni Buddha's time, many followers became arhats. Others asked these enlightened people to fully explain Buddhadharma. The arhats could only speak of strange ideas that no one really understood. It didn't matter, since anything the arhats said would have been superfluous.

There is nothing to say about enlightenment, yet here I am talking about it. Perhaps you're saying to yourself, "I think I'm getting it now. I'm on to something. It won't be long now." Entertaining such thoughts is a mistake.

On his first retreat with me, one practitioner had so many outbursts, I asked him to leave because he was disturbing the others. He reapplied for another retreat and I accepted him on condition that he would control himself. On the fifth day, he thought he had an enlightenment experience. He demanded to see me but I was out in the garden. He walked up to the person in charge and slapped him in the face. Then he approached me and said, "Shifu (honorific for "teacher"), I can go now. I'm enlightened." I made him stay because he was in no condition to go back to normal life. He had nothing more than a strong emotional experience and interpreted it as enlightenment. These are the dangers of relying on knowledge and imagination to guide one's practice.

Enlightenment definitely is possible; otherwise all of Buddhism would be a lie. But if you think you are enlightened and still cling to ideas and feelings, then you are not really enlightened. There is enlightenment and there is also wisdom, but when you try to use wisdom to investigate an enlightenment experience, you will discover that there is no such thing as enlightenment. You cannot say there is no wisdom or attainment, but an enlightened person knows that enlightenment and wisdom have no genuine existence.

The middle of the *Heart Sutra* says, "There is no wisdom and no attainment." A few lines later the sutra seems to contradict itself, saying that a person who understands this attains ultimate enlightenment. This seems strange, but the sutra is talking about different attitudes—one of seeking, one of non-seeking.

In *Substance itself is empty and obscure*, "substance" refers to enlightenment and wisdom, while "empty" means that enlightenment is without attributes: you cannot say that it is this or that. Any description would limit the substance of enlightenment. Why "obscure"? Because the substance is not something you can hear, see, or touch, but at the same time, everything you hear, see, and touch is that substance. A rough analogy would be our relationship to air; although we cannot see, hear, or grasp air, we live in the midst of it.

These two lines affirm that there is wisdom and enlightenment, but we cannot attach to them and we should not seek them. We should not entertain the idea that enlightenment and wisdom are attainable. If there is anything you should seek from practice, it should be to live your life better, more energetically and clearly, and to be at peace with yourself.

This is a real and concrete goal to shoot for. Aiming for enlightenment is foolhardy; you will lose before you even begin. People tell me that they practice to achieve enlightenment; and though they come on retreats and study the Dharma, their lives are a mess. They say they still lose control, that their priorities are wrong, that their attitude toward practice needs fixing. With a change of attitude, plus proper practice and guidance, their lives will become clearer and purer.

If we understand that nothing in this world, including enlightenment, has any real existence, is there anything that we cannot let go of? It might sound easy, but moving to this higher level requires great effort. Fruition is not important, but effort is. If practitioners had such drive and determination to become enlightened, they would live their lives in a diligent and pure manner, and they would be content.

Someone asked today if she could use the method of looking at the mind. But which mind are you looking at—scattered mind or clear mind? One always begins with scattered mind, and there are methods for watching the coming and going of thoughts in the scattered mind. On the other hand, if you want to look directly at your clear mind, there is no difference between clear and scattered mind. However, if you see the mind, know that it is not your clear mind that you see.

We can look at and analyze the scattered mind and we can do the same with unified mind, but the enlightened mind cannot be seen or examined by knowledge. We can say that clear mind is the same as no-mind, but how can you look at no-mind?

3.2 ■ Did the Method Leave You?

> Thoughts arise and pass away,
> The preceding no different from the
> succeeding.

The *Song* says, *Thoughts arise and pass away.* This is from the point of view of the scattered mind of ordinary sentient beings. Therefore, this is where we must begin, with ordinary scattered mind. In the ordinary mind thoughts are succeeded by new thoughts in a continuous stream.

In the state we call samadhi the flow of thoughts has ceased, but the constant march of thought resumes when the power of samadhi subsides. To bring thinking to a halt, or at least to slow it down, we use a thought to watch other thoughts; we use a consciously picked thought to watch succeeding thoughts rise and fall. The point is to become clearly aware of the rise and fall of thoughts as they occur. If we are aware and exercise will power, there is less opportunity for wandering thoughts to pull us off the method.

For example, in breath counting, three thoughts occur in a cycle: the thought of the self, the thought of the self counting, and the thought of the number. To use the method properly, at the very least, these three thoughts must arise one after the other. When you continuously connect these three thoughts like links in a chain, other thoughts have no room to interrupt your flow of awareness. If there are only these three thoughts in your mind, you will have no sense of time or space; the breath will be smooth and the body will feel light. In this manner you will eventually enter samadhi, where even the counting ceases.

Attaining an unbroken chain of awareness is the goal for all methods of meditation, not just breath counting. The problem is that most of us cannot do it for a long time. For instance, sleepiness will cause the chain to break up like tiny fragments floating in the sky, or even disappear altogether.

3.3 ▪ Collecting the Scattered Mind

> If the succeeding thought does not arise,
> The preceding thought cuts itself off.

This stanza speaks of thoughts arising and passing, of the preceding thought not being different from the succeeding one, but it has a deeper meaning as well. In the enlightened mind thoughts also rise and fall, but there is no discrimination, no attachment toward one thought and aversion toward the other—all are experienced with equanimity. A woman is a woman; a man is a man; gold is gold; a rock is a rock. Thoughts are just as they are, without evoking accompanying emotions; this allows the enlightened mind to deal directly and equally with all preceding and succeeding thoughts.

We are aware of a thought because a new thought arises and replaces it. Successive thoughts enable us to be aware of our previous thoughts. If you are counting breaths and your mind settles on the thought of "one" and does not move, then there is no conception at all; you will not be aware of any thoughts, including the number one. On the other hand, if thoughts of the same number arise and replace themselves over and over, then awareness of the number will remain. This is true for any thought. If your mind stops on a thought, then you will be unaware of that thought. For example, thinking of killing something is wrong, but if your mind stops on a thought of killing and nothing comes after it, then the thought of killing loses its meaning. Therefore, if a thought arises and no other thoughts come after it, the first thought will disappear.

The purpose of a method of practice is to collect the scattered mind and thus unify it. When you are practicing correctly and well, the three thoughts—self, self counting, and number—remain in an ongoing cycle. Eventually the method should leave you, but it does not work the other way around; in other words, you should not purposely leave the method.

If the method naturally and spontaneously leaves you, that is good— it means that the three thoughts have reduced to one, that of the self. In this state you are no longer aware of a number, the breath, or a method. Even if you are aware of breathing, you will be unable to count breaths. The method has not left you. Rather, it has accomplished its purpose, which was to bring your mind to one thought: awareness of self. In fact, you are still on the method and your mind is clear, calm, and tranquil; it is definitely not blank.

Some practitioners hear me talk of the method going away, and they think they should be at that point already, so they stop using the method. I ask them whether the method left them, or they left the method. There is a big difference. If you have dropped the method, I advise you strongly to pick it up again. If the method dropped you, in fact it has not; it is still there, so there is nothing to pick up again.

The two lines of the stanza above describe enlightenment, but not necessarily samadhi. In shallow samadhi there are still subtle thoughts, as well as feelings of happiness and pleasure. In deeper samadhi the mind naturally stays on one thought; the previous thought does not need to cut itself off. Enlightenment is different from samadhi in that there is no attachment or aversion to any particular thought; so there is no need for one thought to succeed another.

Here is an analogy. As monkeys climb, three of their limbs usually support them while the fourth extends to climb. As the fourth limb moves, the other three soon follow. If the monkey has no intention of climbing further, the fourth limb stops and the other three limbs also rest. There is no subsequent movement of any limb. In the same way, if the mind does not anticipate a following thought, then the previous thoughts and attachments naturally disappear.

Someone told me that they needed a good way to combat vexations. There is no need to combat vexations. If while meditating you are aware of vexations, just return to the method. Once you are aware of them, vexations begin to lose their power. For example, once you realize that you are angry, the emotion usually subsides. Thoughts, emotions, and feelings persist because succeeding thoughts replace previous thoughts. If the anger persists, that is because you attach to that anger, thus producing subsequent thoughts of anger. When you are truly and clearly aware of your anger, it will diminish.

When vexations arise, do not struggle or run with them; letting them go is the best method. If you were tempted to steal something and thought, "I know it's wrong, but I wonder what it would be like to steal. Let me try it. I'll worry about it later." That is running with vexation. These thoughts can continue for some time because you are attached to the vexation. If the attachment is strong you may finally act on your thoughts. If, on the other hand, you don't attach to the idea of stealing, the thought will go away.

No Thought, No Mind, Equals Enlightenment

> In past, present and future, there is nothing;
> No mind, no buddha.

Buddhadharma says there is no past, present, or future. There is also no vexation, no mind, no enlightenment, and no buddha. In the original Chinese, *past, present, and future* are referred to as "the three worlds." The phrase can also refer to past, present, and future lives, but this is not what Niutou is talking about. He is in fact referring to the previous, present, and future thoughts. If the previous thought is gone, and the next thought has not yet arisen, that is precisely no-thought, or no-mind. If there is no thought, there is also no vexation, no enlightenment, and no buddha. When we are vexed, or when we seek enlightenment, we entertain thoughts. When we have no thoughts, we also have no mind, and that is enlightenment.

Still, we speak of enlightenment and buddhahood. If we didn't, no one would be inspired to practice. That is why I urge everyone to attain buddhahood. For us, enlightenment exists and is something to strive for, but for enlightened ones, there is no enlightenment. The *Song* speaks from the stance of enlightenment, but when we practice our point of view is that there is no such thing.

For some, these ideas may be very abstract. Here you are grappling with sleepiness and scattered minds, and I am talking about there being no past, present, or future. The sleepiness will pass, but a scattered mind dwells in the past and the future, never in the present moment. If we use a string to represent time, one end being past and the other being future, where do we place the present? Really, there is no present moment along that string that we can isolate. As soon as we hold the present up to inspection, it is already in the past. If we look for a moment to arrive, it is still in the future. The past is gone, the future is not yet. Neither exists. All that exists is the present moment, yet we cannot point to it. If we limit the present moment to the smallest amount of time, it disappears into nothingness. From the point of view of this nonexistent present moment, only the past and the future remain. Therefore, we say that the present moment is also in the past and future, and has no real existence either.

What I speak of is a continuum of past, present, and future. When you say your back hurts, it is already in the past, and you anticipate future pain. But if the pain is in the past and future, why bother with it? Of course, this is easier said than done. We are still aware of pain, and it seems to be in the present moment. Working on this understanding is practice. It is a method with which to approach pain, or anything else for that matter.

Whatever vexations you may have, use this method: see things clearly as being in the past, present, and future, then see that the past and future do not exist. But if nothing is there, how can there be vexation? It is difficult to separate from pain and vexation, but I never said practice was easy. Neither is it complicated; you don't have to watch every vexation, and apply the "past, present, and future" test to it. Just stay on the method. When the mind is completely and smoothly on the method, it will eventually disappear by itself. It may seem as if you are not practicing, but in fact, this is true practice.

I have been wearing these eyeglasses for so many years, I am sometimes not aware they are on my face. Some doctors say that a good sign of health is a feeling of lightness. When your body feels heavy, it is a sign that maybe something is wrong. It is the same with practice. If the method is smooth and the mind light, it seems as if there is no work to be done, nothing to be gained, and nothing to lose. This is practice at its best: relaxed and light with no expectations.

People come to retreat hoping to gain something or to get rid of something. They want to gain miraculous physical improvements, to solve longtime problems, or to rid themselves of vexation. Many find some success, but their attitude is wrong. They come with heavy minds and bodies and leave the same way. Unless you have a real health problem, do not concern yourself with your body during retreat. Do not concern yourself with what happened before the retreat and what will happen afterward. Put your mind on the present in the most pleasant and down-to-earth manner you can muster. This is practicing without using your mind. When you practice without using your mind, there is no idea of attaining buddhahood; there is only practice.

3.4 ■ From Caterpillar to Buddha

> Sentient beings are without mind;
> Out of no-mind they manifest.

The mind of a buddha and the mind of sentient beings are the same. If they were not, it would be impossible for sentient beings to become buddhas. This mind of wisdom can be called pure mind or buddha-mind. Understanding and accepting this principle is the first step in Chan. It builds faith in oneself and the Dharma; it also builds faith in the practice as we turn vexations into buddha-mind.

Under the right conditions, light will reflect off dust particles in the air so that the sun's rays will become visible. If there were no dust motes in the air, you would see sunlight and the objects it falls on, but you would not see the ray of light between them. We think we see sunlight, but what we really see is the dust. It is the same with the mind. When we look at the mind, what we see is the movement of vexations. You think, "I see my mind moving," but in fact you are just looking at your vexations. Does this mean that there is no mind? That would be like saying there is no sunlight if you don't see sunrays. Whether or not there is dust to reflect the sunlight, the sunlight is still there. Likewise, when you have no vexations you will not see your mind functioning, but it still functions. You cannot say the pure mind exists, because there is no way the mind of vexation can observe it. You also cannot say that it does not exist, for buddhas are enlightened and still have minds that function.

Therefore, the difference between the mind of a buddha and the mind of sentient beings is that a buddha's mind has no vexation. However, we must use the mind *of* vexation in order to free our mind *from* vexation. So we collect our scattered mind into a concentrated mind, turn that into one-mind, and finally, one-mind into no-mind. Once no-mind is attained and you have revealed the buddha-mind, there is no practice.

While we must use our minds when we practice, if we remember and attach to good experiences, we are clinging to the mind of vexation. Such expectations create more problems. Therefore, it is best to let go of good experiences no matter how pleasant, deep, or useful. Attaching to and trying to repeat them, one falls into a rut. This is a major obstacle to successful practice.

If you have the same pleasant experience several times, you will probably notice familiar signs that say you are about to have another, and you become expectant. This approach can become a habit—practice becomes a smooth, comfortable ride, and there progress stops. I am not saying that one should avoid good experiences, for that too would be an obstruction. You should not consciously crave nor shun any meditation experience. Just know when you experience something good or bad, that you do not own it. This awareness will remind you that any experience is neither a rest stop nor a destination, and that you should just continue with your practice.

Some practitioners who have been on several retreats easily fall into this rut. They practice hard, have good experiences, and stop there. Retreats become familiar, and repeating these pleasant interludes becomes the goal. They begin to think there is nothing more to practice, and stop pushing forward. Such an attitude indicates that they misunderstand Buddhadharma. It also suggests that they do not practice much between retreats. They likely practice in spurts—work hard on retreats, then pursue other interests in daily life. I am not saying that lay people should live like monks and nuns. By all means, pursue interests, hobbies, and have social lives, but not at the expense of meditation. It is also a good idea to regularly read Buddhist literature so that your understanding of Buddhadharma stays fresh and focused.

Striving to repeat a good experience is using the mind of vexation, and makes it impossible for you to break through your shell of ignorance to see your buddha-nature. You will remain entangled in a web of vexations.

> Distinguishing between profane and sacred,
> Their vexations flourish.

I am an ordinary sentient being and teach my students to view themselves the same way. We are not sages. I know I am distinguishing between *profane and sacred*, but I do so for good reasons. First, genuine sages rarely claim they are enlightened. Even Chan patriarchs made no such claims. Claiming sagehood is a sure sign that one is not a sage. Second, it is not easy to recognize a sage. Those who claim sagehood are often ordinary people who have just mastered a few impressive skills. The safest approach is to think of yourself as an ordinary person and not worry about becoming a sage.

Judging yourself with criteria appropriate for a sage spells trouble. It is bad enough to think you are wise, but misleading others is worse. There is also the opposite problem—seeing what it takes to be a sage, you may become discouraged. All around, you see diligent practitioners who appear to be bodhisattvas. You imagine yourself a blemish in a blessed environment, a rat in a meadow full of beautiful rabbits. In disillusionment you may even give up practicing. You should think of yourself neither as a blemished rat nor as a pure, beautiful rabbit that doesn't need to practice anymore. Just see yourself as an ordinary practitioner.

The emphasis in practice should be on the process, not the result. It is good to have goals, but when you get down to practice, put goals aside and just practice. Practice is like taking a trip: you and other travelers come to the same airport to start their journeys. Each flight has its own departure time, destination, and arrival time. You buy your ticket, settle into your seat, and they into theirs. Once you are en route, there is no point worrying about the route or arrival time. Eventually, you will arrive at your destination, as does everyone else.

On a twenty-three-hour flight from New York to Taiwan, we had stopovers in Alaska and Korea. The man next to me complained, "I should have used the other airline. Its flight was only sixteen hours."

"Fine," I said, "go back to New York and take that other flight."

"I can't do that, it's too late, and it would take even more time."

So I said, "In that case, there's no point discussing it any further."

A Chinese aphorism says that once you're on a pirate ship, you may as well become a pirate. In other words, as a practitioner, do not look back. You are already en route—just get on with your practice. Don't compare yourself with others. Having their own causes and conditions, people will naturally find their own paths and have their own experiences. As you practice, your causes and conditions will change, and so will your experiences. Do not concern yourself with the results of your practice; they too will come and go and change. Just being concerned with the present moment is the best and safest way to practice.

A young girl thought she was ugly. Her mother told her, "Don't worry, when you are eighteen, you will be beautiful." Years passed and on her eighteenth birthday, the girl looked into the mirror and still didn't like what she saw. Her mother said, "You are so much more beautiful than when you were a little girl; you just don't realize it. A puppy who grows into a large dog is still a dog, and a duckling will not turn into a swan."

The point of this story is this: as you practice, do you worry about your progress? If you tend to belittle yourself like the girl in the story, remember that each moment is a new beginning, a fresh start. Practice is forever beginning, so don't think in terms of time. Forget about being a veteran with years of experience under your belt. For a caterpillar to become a butterfly, it must first crawl, eat leaves, and become a cocoon for a long time. Rushing cannot make it become a butterfly any quicker. Like a caterpillar, we must take time to mature naturally. Again and again I say, do not look for success or fear failure. Just practice. If you can practice diligently on this retreat, that is already success.

Making Progress in Waves

> Splitting hairs deviates from the eternal.
> Seeking the real, you give up the true.

Splitting hairs means making comparisons and distinctions, like comparing yourself with others, your present with your past or an imagined future, the good with the bad. Making such distinctions, you stray from the right path. People usually split hairs over minor things, but making distinctions of any kind is obstructive. A single thought that you can't let go of is also an obstruction. Whatever your mind dwells on is subject to change, while a true principle does not.

Progress in practice is not steady and linear; it is more like a wave, sometimes going up, sometimes going down. A good day can be followed by a horrible day, and vice versa. It can even change from sitting to sitting, from moment to moment. If you always perceive things as getting worse and worse, you have a mind of comparison. You will be making trouble for yourself, and may become disillusioned; you may lose faith in yourself, in the practice, and in the Dharma. When it comes to practice, making comparisons and distinctions only leads to problems.

Practice is influenced by many factors, including one's physical condition, which can go through cycles. You are not always in control or even aware of these cycles. What seems like regression may actually be a dip in physiological function. In the midst of a down cycle you may see only negativity—there is nothing to look forward to. But if you took a long view, you would see up-and-down, wavelike progress over the years. I asked a young practitioner how her practice was going.

"Horrible. It can't get any worse."

I said, "In that case it can only get better. Congratulations!"

Recognizing the up-and-down nature of progress is important. Because you go through many states of mind, enduring the cycles requires resolve. As long as you are diligent and consistent in practice, there is no need to compare today with the past, or with an imagined future. Just practice according to your capacity without becoming obsessed. Practice like a fine stream that runs smoothly and continuously, not like a flood which comes all at once, does a lot of damage, and disappears. That is not a good way to expend your energy.

Some people practice a particular method their entire lives and never see any marked results or progress. Did they waste their time? Definitely not. During the time when one works hard without seeing tangible results, effort is not being wasted. Even if you die without becoming enlightened, you will have planted good karmic seeds for your next life. Practice should become a routine like brushing your teeth. Don't worry about what good it is doing. You will be benefiting greatly whether you notice it or not.

There is a famous gong'an in which a monk asked Chan Master Zhaozhou, "Does a dog have buddha-nature?" and Master Zhaozhou answered, "*Wu*," meaning "no" or "without." If you turn Zhaozhou's answer into a *huatou*, it becomes "What is *wu*?" If you practice this *huatou*, even to your very last breath, you will have gained many benefits.

There is also a Chan allegory about a monk who was not enlightened, but who practiced this same *huatou* his whole life. When the monk was dying, the king of the underworld sent two demons to capture the unenlightened monk's mind while he was still alive. But even though he was dying, the monk kept practicing his *huatou*: "What is *wu*?" Because the monk's mind was completely on the *huatou*, the ghosts were not able to capture it. They went back and informed the demon king, who said, "I don't know the answer to the question, but we should leave this monk alone." The point is, whether or not you become enlightened, practice benefits you.

People may ask, "What is the use in counting my breath over and over?" The answer is that this method trains your mind. If you always return to your method after losing count, wandering thoughts will not rule your mind. So long as you are practicing sufficiently well, even if not perfectly, you have a lifeline. If you slip a little, you will be able to grab hold again. Right below there could be a deep abyss, but you won't fall to the bottom; you will always be able to grab the lifeline and climb back up.

Someone here practiced a mantra believing it beneficial, but switched to breath counting because he thought he could get better results. To look for better results in another method is a mistake. Standing on top of a mountain looking at a higher mountain, you may think you should be on that higher mountain. It can be like this in practice. You may feel that you are not having enough success, and you want to reach a higher peak, but as soon as you make these kinds of discriminations, right away you drift off your practice.

Seeking the real, you turn away from the true, says that in seeking enlightenment, you are moving further away from it. If a feather is floating in the air, and you try to suddenly grab it, disturbing the air will make the feather float farther away. If you have expectation in your practice and try to seize a goal, it will recede from you.

3.5 ▪ Getting Rid of Problems Is a Problem

> Discarding both is the cure,
> Transparent, bright, pure.

There are two kinds of obstructions in practice; one is trying to get rid of problems that come up, the other is thinking that there are no problems. In the first situation, trying to get rid of problems can lead to exhaustion and vexation. Recall the line we talked about the other night,

Distinguishing between profane and sacred, vexations flourish. If you try to get rid of vexations, that in itself is a vexation. Trying to get rid of wandering thoughts is just adding another wandering thought.

Today somebody's nose itched, as if there was a very fine feather in his nostril, and he kept telling himself, "No, I am not going to bother with this." The more he told himself that, the more his nose itched. Eventually he came to me with his problem and I gave him some Tiger Balm. However, if this person could have concentrated more on the method instead of worrying about the itching, it would have been less of a distraction.

When my legs hurt when I sit, I just let them ache and do not stir. After a while the pain turns into a cool sensation. If I stir a bit, the pain may return, so I just remain still and continue like this. Later on I can move my legs so they do not hurt. With this kind of training, you can sit for much longer periods. However, it is possible only for people with very strong determination and will power. When it's hurting a lot, saying, "OK, I will put my concentration on the method" won't work if you just cannot transfer your attention, or summon up the energy. At this point, all you can do is keep your attention on your pain and bear with it.

Do not try to get rid of the routine pains that come up in practice. You can just accept them, or focus on the method. If you can do either of these the pain will eventually go away by itself. Sometimes pain comes if you are not relaxed enough. Pain may also come from an injury that you are not aware of. Your circulation will improve during meditation, so the energy may be getting to these injured areas, which is good. When possible, it is better to accept pain rather than run from it. In acupuncture, if the needle is put at the right spot relative to your problem, and you react to that, chances are the needle is indeed in the right spot. However, if the needle has not been inserted in the right place, there may be no such response. In a similar way pain can indicate that something good is happening when you are meditating.

Another obstruction is people thinking they have no problem, when in fact they have a very big one. When this happens, it is very difficult to make real progress in practice. They need a master they trust to tell them,

"Yes, you have a big problem, and the problem is that you don't recognize it." Lacking such advice, a person can go on like this for a very long time. While practicing he has very little vexation, but in daily life he still has a lot of vexation. Awareness may be all it takes to solve the problem, but it may be a long time before recognition comes. It would be easier and quicker if he had a good teacher who can point out his problems.

If you have wandering thoughts, it's all right so long as you are aware of them. What is bad is not recognizing them and thinking, "I really had a good time this afternoon, thinking about all sorts of things." Having wandering thoughts is not a problem, but not recognizing them is. Some sitters get into subtle levels of thinking because their mind is much clearer and calmer, while others get lost in pleasant thoughts. These people may not be aware that they have a problem.

There was a lay person in Taiwan who used to write poetry, but then lost the inspiration. When he became a monk late in life, he started writing poetry again. His master asked him, "How come you're writing poetry again?" The monk said, "I am grateful to you master, for teaching me meditation. When I meditate now, the poetry just starts flowing." If this is what he gets out of meditation, this monk has a problem.

The meaning of the line, *Transparent, bright, pure*, is that if there is no specific problem to address, enlightenment will manifest. Someone told me today, "I've been waiting, waiting, and waiting. My mind is very silent, very quiet. If I sit in this silence, will I eventually get to no-mind?"

I said, "This quiescence is different from no-mind. However, if you continue in this direction, it's possible to get to no-mind, and sometimes you get there without realizing it. Nonetheless, no-mind is different from just quiescence. In the state of quiescence, you sense your mind being very tranquil. Therefore, there's still that thought in your mind. The state of no-mind is equally tranquil and quiescent, but there is no thought."

No need for hard work or skill

4.1 ■ Be Like an Infant

> No need for hard work or skill;
> Keep to the actions of an infant.

It is odd that we are at these lines of the poem just now. This morning I talked about being like a newborn infant when you come to retreat. Somebody asked, "If we are infants, where are our diapers?" A new baby doesn't need to know anything about diapers; that is the mother's job. The same thing applies to you. Everything you know, everything you have learned before, you don't need here. Just be like a new baby when you practice. People might think that the purpose in life is to learn more and more, and that Niutou is giving us strange advice here. Isn't what he is telling us something to learn? Yes but once we learn it we should just put it away.

How many eyelashes do you have? It's right there on your face, yet you probably don't know. Even if you knew, can that knowledge be useful? In daily life it is correct to use knowledge, but where practice is concerned, a lot of knowledge can be a distraction. If you come to retreat wanting to learn a lot, then you won't; if you think you already know a lot, you won't make much progress. The ideal is to be like an infant.

Some people practice with me for eight to ten years, and then ask me what level they are at. When I tell them they are still beginners, some will say, "If I'm a beginner, what about those people just starting out?" I say, "They are beginners to themselves and you are a beginner to yourself. If you ask me fifty years from now, I will still say you are a beginner." Do you understand?

Question: Are you still a beginner, Shifu?

Sheng Yen: Yes, I'm still a beginner, always a beginner. Why a beginner? Because I never learn.

Student: I can be like an infant, but I still have the consciousness of an adult.

Sheng Yen: That's right. You want to be *like* an infant, but you don't want to really *be* an infant. You still need to use a method; you still read sutras and listen to lectures. If you were really an infant, you couldn't do these things or understand me. Being *like* an infant means having no ideas of right or wrong, good or bad, and no conception of progress or no progress. So, if you have ideas like striving to succeed or being afraid of failure, where do you think you'll end up?

Richard here has been practicing very hard but he just feels that he hasn't made progress. I was watching him and he had a very determined expression. After observing him for some time with that expression, I thought I'd better have an interview with him. I called him into the interview room and advised him to relax. Practice should always start in a relaxed manner without seeking any benefit, without looking for progress. If you can begin like that, you'll move forward quickly.

Suppose you were in a desert without water and the only chance you had to survive was to start digging until you uncovered a spring. Assuming the hole you dig is likely to produce water, if you dig too hastily you may get exhausted and die before you get to water. Practice is a little like digging for water in a desert. It's urgent that you find water, but you can't rush it.

Someone said today, "I try very hard, but every time I try to count to ten, all I get to is five, and I have to go back to one again. I couldn't even get past five."

I told him, "If you had not been counting your breath, you would not have realized that you couldn't count past five. So now you know how scattered your mind is, and that's useful." At what age is a child able to count to ten?

Student: Two or three.

Sheng Yen: And here we are grown up, not able to count to ten. Of course you're all like infants so it's understandable. Even so you should be happy and enthusiastic. If you let yourself get overanxious, you'll get to the count of two and then get lost. And finally you'll end up saying, "Forget it. I used to be smart, now I'm stupid. What kind of practice is this?"

If you feel useless or unable to work well on any method, it is very easy to become discouraged. Please don't fear failure. As far as practice is concerned, there's no such thing as failure. Discomfort is normal; drowsiness is normal; lack of focus is also normal. I deceive people—I tell them that three days into the retreat their legs and back will no longer hurt, and they'll be very concentrated. This is actually true because the first three days are harsher. By the fourth day people have usually adapted to some extent, and then they don't have too many problems.

Still, during the first couple of days people often think about going home. Anyone thinking about leaving today? You? Anyone else? Maybe tomorrow there will be some more. And by the third day maybe fewer people, and then by the fourth day nobody will want to go home.

In any case, you should not change your method at will. First ask me about it. I can guide you if I know your problem. However, if you don't tell me about your problems and just leave, I cannot help you.

No Shortcut to Enlightenment

> Clearly knowing,
> The net of views increases

When we start practicing, we see things the way normal people do—mountains are mountains and rivers are rivers. After we are deep into the practice, mountains are no longer mountains, and rivers are no longer rivers. This will happen when you are practicing very single-mindedly, and people may even perceive you as a little foggy. At this stage you may not even recognize yourself in the mirror. When you finally attain enlightenment, you once again see that mountains are mountains and rivers are rivers.

In the beginning we see things according to our attachments and feelings. In a good mood we see mountains and rivers as beautiful, but in a bad mood things can change. Once I was hiking up a mountain with some people. When we started out everybody was in high spirits: "Look at this beautiful mountain. You don't see anything like this in the city." After about three hours, some people's mood began to change, and the beautiful mountains became annoying: "Are we ever going to get to the top of this mountain?"

If an enlightened person were on that trip, how would he see that mountain? From the start he sees the mountain just as it is. He knows he has to climb to the summit, however high. On the way he feels no elation or aversion. He always feels the same, either way.

The other day a woman came to me crying. Her kids are growing up, and her husband has been treating her very badly. When they first got married he was very good to her, but after seven or eight years they fought a lot, and there is talk of divorce. She wanted my advice. I advised her not to get divorced.

She said, "It's not my husband who wants a divorce, it's me."

I asked her, "Have you ever eaten sugar cane?"

"Yes."

"When you eat sugar cane, which end do you start chewing on?"

She asked, "What's the difference? Aren't both ends the same?"

I said, "No, they're not. The root end of the cane is very sweet, but when you get to the leaf end it's nearly tasteless. You might as well drink water. If you start opposite the root, as you approach the root, it gets sweeter. Your relationship with your husband right now is like being at the far end of the cane. If you start there and work toward the root of your problems with your husband, things will get better. Just because it's not that sweet right now, don't just throw your marriage away."

Practice is like this. Everybody understand? If you're not doing well you may think, "This is a waste of time. I'm practicing without pleasure and involvement." With this attitude the possibility is that it's going to get worse. The less you discriminate about your own situation, the better you can practice.

There were two sisters who didn't know very much about their husbands before they got married. One sister thought she wanted someone strong and forceful, while the other thought she wanted somebody gentle. However, the one who wanted a forceful husband ended up marrying someone gentle, and vice versa. As it turned out, each sister was happy with the man she married. What each thought she wanted was not really what she needed. Likewise, when you're practicing, let go of preconceptions such as, "If I take this little shortcut, I'll get enlightened faster." What you want may not be what you need. There's no shortcut to enlightenment.

Provided you are persistent and diligent, the more difficult practice is, the better the results. Looking for shortcuts won't gain you power nor get you very far. The denser your "net of views," the more difficult it will be to attain liberation. Knowledge about Buddhist methods is useful, but when you're practicing do not try to use that knowledge to figure out how to practice well. Your "net of views" will just tighten around you. Keep to the method and work diligently, without worrying about the past or the future. Otherwise, what should be a straightforward path becomes a whole lot of useless side trips. Put down your former knowledge and opinions about practice, and put your mind on the method. Definitely do not think about gong'ans and koans (Jap. for gong'an), about what some Buddhist term means, or anything like that. Forget all that and be like an infant.

4.2 ▧ True Stillness Is Samadhi

> Stillness without seeing,
> Not moving in a dark room.
>
> Wakeful without wandering,
> The mind is tranquil yet bright.

Some practitioners mistake samadhi for enlightenment. This is what Niutou refers to by Stillness without seeing. The author implies that having an unmoving mind that does not function is like sitting motionless in a dark room. By contrast, the second couplet describes the enlightened mind: awake but not wandering, tranquil, yet bright. These words are often used to describe the enlightened mind, which is still and clear, yet functions. In terms of our practice, "wakeful" refers to contemplation and "tranquil" alludes to stillness.

We should see the methods of contemplation as observing our thoughts with a still or tranquil mind. For beginners this means that the mind should be relaxed, just observing without thinking. Can you do this? Can you do slow-walking meditation without your mind wandering? Do you command your body to walk or does your body walk by itself? And if you are not thinking while you walk, who is it that walks?

True stillness, or stopping, is samadhi. In the beginning, stillness means not thinking about anything other than your method. When you get to the point where you contemplate one thing only, that is one-mind. When the mind is single-minded and not moving, it is the same as stillness. This is the objective of contemplation in the beginning stages: to still the mind.

At this time I would say that most of us cannot still our minds. As we contemplate we also entertain other thoughts, and even if we arrive at stillness, it is weak and tenuous. Unless your contemplation is deep and your will strong, you will soon waver from stillness. To rein in your scattered mind, you will have to pick up contemplation again. It is normal to weave between stillness and being scattered, so please do not yield to frustration.

To enter samadhi you must bring your mind to one point. Everything but the method must disappear, and eventually that should, too. In practice, you can be clearly aware of phenomena and still remain relatively unmoved by them. The feeling may even persist after meditating. This is a good experience, especially for beginners, and useful in daily life, but it is not the path to samadhi.

Some practitioners reach a point where they are not using their minds, and moreover, are not in a knowing or aware state. This is neither samadhi nor the road to samadhi. It is like being locked in a dark room. This is blankness, not true samadhi in which there is no sense of time or space and no awareness of self. In the stillness described by the *Song*, the tranquil awareness of self, time, and space is different from both samadhi and enlightenment.

When you think that you are in samadhi, you are not. When you return from true samadhi you will feel differently from how you normally feel, but there will be no announcement that you have just experienced samadhi. People experiencing samadhi are clear and relaxed, not un-knowing idiots. If to become idiotic were the goal of meditation, there would not be many followers.

Make Your Mind Like a Mirror

Wakeful without wandering and *tranquil yet bright* is the correct way to be when practicing. You are clear about what you are doing and what is happening around you, yet you have no scattered thoughts, and are not influenced by anything going on. You hear people walking and talking outside the Chan Center, but your mind does not fix or rest on that. When they are gone your mind does not follow them. Like a mirror, your mind clearly reflects what is in front of it, but when the object passes the mirror is again empty. Make your mind like a mirror, not like a camera. A camera captures a moment, freezes it, and stores it on film. If your mind is like a camera, constantly receiving and holding onto in-formation, it is a hindrance to practice.

All thoughts are ultimately wandering thoughts, but this is how the discriminating mind works. To dispel the mind of discrimination and illusion, we use discrimination and illusion. Hence, methods like count-ing breaths and reciting mantras are themselves wandering thoughts, but they are correct wandering thoughts for what we are trying to do. All thoughts other than the method are extraneous as well as wandering, but dealing harshly with them is not an effective strategy. Once aware that you have abandoned your method in favor of a wandering thought, just disengage yourself from the thought and return to the method. Then you will have returned to a "correct" wandering thought, that is, the method.

We have a garden behind the Chan Center. We pull out the weeds for the sake of the flowers and vegetables, but we do not become annoyed at the weeds. Weeds are natural and inevitable, and we should thank them because they help us maintain a healthy and beautiful garden. Wandering thoughts are like weeds in the garden, not to be cursed. They help to strengthen our concentration and resolve.

When the mind is tranquil and devoid of wandering thoughts, it will be clear and bright. In Florida I visited Seaworld and looked through a glass wall at an underwater environment. Because the water was so still, it was as if there was no water there at all. This is how our minds should be—clear but unmoving. That is not yet samadhi, but you will naturally experience this unmoving clarity on the way.

The enlightened mind is different from both the mind that experiences samadhi and the mind that is scattered. After enlightenment, people are not in samadhi, but their mind is like that of someone in samadhi. Enlightened beings are involved in everyday activities, but their minds do not give rise to attraction or aversion. This can be considered the samadhi power that derives from enlightenment. However, most enlightenment experiences are not permanent; eventually, the samadhi power will fade. How long it lasts depends on the depth of the realization.

The difference between one who experiences samadhi with enlightenment, and one who experiences samadhi without enlightenment, is that the former has seen the intrinsic buddha-nature. I must be clear here because I am talking about samadhi in two different contexts. First is the samadhi power that arises when one has cultivated a truly stable mind. This power can derive from samadhi or enlightenment. Samadhi also describes a level of meditative absorption where the mind stops on one thought and everything else disappears.

Most realizations of enlightenment fade over time. For most people it is a flash of recognition that comes and goes. After that they must redouble their efforts to cultivate realization. On the other hand, while a truly great realization is rare, it does not fade. The best example of this is the great enlightenment of the Buddha himself.

The minds of enlightened beings are like mirrors responding spontaneously to sentient beings through the function of wisdom. However, enlightened beings do not perceive an enlightened "I" that helps people. A mirror is not conscious of what it reflects. Ordinary sentient beings attach great importance to certain things and reject others, but enlightened beings see everything as being equal. They are aware that sentient beings suffer, but they no longer experience it themselves. They respond to us with compassion, not sympathy. To some, enlightened beings seem too detached from what makes us human. Many people would not want to be so dispassionate. Because of desire we have emotions and vexations, and because of desire we suffer. Therefore, it is impossible to understand what it is like to be without desire. We project our experience and feelings onto this imagined enlightenment, and perceive it to be empty and negative. We cling to our emotions as if they truly define us.

As long as one is attached to a self-center, one cannot realize enlightenment; so don't waste time fearing that enlightenment will turn you into a block of wood. Do not be concerned with what the illusory mind cannot understand. When you have such wandering thoughts, just return to the wandering thought that is your practice.

4.3 ▪ To a Buddha, There Is No Buddhahood

> All phenomena are real and eternal,
> Profuse, yet of a single form.

These lines describe the mind after enlightenment. Before enlightenment, phenomena are illusory—neither eternal nor real. When we imagine and discriminate, the worldly ideas and knowledge we accumulate are not ultimate. But in daily life, most people would say that what they perceive is real. Yesterday someone told me about a lifelong curiosity about things. Most people are naturally inquisitive. Being curious is how we learn, and we usually take what we learn to be "real."

We argue because we think we are right and the other party is wrong. Some people are even willing to fight for what they believe in. Our inability to harmonize our minds or attention stems from our attachment to our attitudes and ideas. This can lead to conflict with others and even within ourselves.

Yesterday I asked you to forget the past and future and just work on the present moment. When I noticed someone sitting in a slumped, slack manner, I asked him what was wrong. He said he was waiting for his energy to rise. I left him alone and by the next sitting his energy level was up; he straightened up and began to practice hard. This morning when he did the same thing, I told him that yesterday was yesterday, and today is today, and to let go of the past. What worked then will not likely work now.

Your body and mind are in constant flux. Attaching to what happened in the past and expecting it to happen again will likely create vexations. The expectant mind rarely gets what it expects. Here is a fable to explain what I mean. One day a fisherman caught a large fish. Some time later, remembering his earlier luck, he returned to the same spot on the river. In the interim a pier had been built precisely over where he fished the last time. Nonetheless he cast his line onto the pier and waited for the fish to bite. His expectation caused him to believe in an illusion.

When things happen, at that moment they are real, but attaching to the experience is illusory. Things come and go like lightning. Today, someone told me that while he was meditating, he had a clear vision that he had killed someone in a past life. I told him that it was an illusion. He asked if all things that happened in the past were illusions. I told him that the events were real when they happened, but they are illusions when they occur as memories. It is important to realize that things are real when they are happening. If everything were illusory no one would practice, for that too would be illusory. The idea of practice is illusory, but practice itself is not, because when you practice correctly, you deal with the present moment.

This same person also asked if liberation was also an illusion. I said that the concept of liberation is illusory, and thinking oneself liberated is also illusory. However, liberation itself is not. If it were, there would be no point in practicing. There would also be no point in doing anything: you could do anything you wanted because any consequence would also be illusory.

Today a construction crew was fixing a gas pipe next door. All day we heard people talking, machines operating, jackhammers going. Now it is quiet. If your mind is still echoing with the noise, you are clinging to the past. If you take it to bed with you, you won't be able to sleep. This is clearly illusory. On the other hand, if an argument during the day keeps you awake, its illusory nature might not be as clear.

This is easier said than done. In practice, if you can view phenomena as unreal, they will be easier to put down. Today someone wept loudly.

Did anyone think, "What's wrong with her? Is Shifu going to help her? Should I help her, or should I just continue meditating?" If you thought this way, your busy mind made several turns in a few seconds. Her crying was real, but the thoughts in your mind triggered by her crying would have been illusory.

Buddhas and bodhisattvas compassionately help sentient beings without themselves being affected. Some people may see buddhas and bodhisattvas as heartless, but such a view stems from attachment to an idea of self. Buddhas and bodhisattvas perceive no separation between themselves and sentient beings. Thus they do not perceive sentient beings as individuals. If there were such a thing as a separate self, then there would indeed be sentient beings, and if there were separate sentient beings, there would definitely be a self.

If you dwell on the idea of enlightenment, it will only elude you. Once enlightened, you will not dwell on it anyway. If you did, it would mean you are not really enlightened. Likewise, do not entertain thoughts of achieving buddhahood. To buddhas, there is no buddhahood.

For now, let go of attachments and practice without thought of gaining. This will take care of the future. As soon as I tell you that you are doing well it will be in the past, so let that go also. If I criticize your diligence, do not chastise yourself. Just take my advice and continue practicing.

Good and Bad Come and Go

> Going, coming, sitting, standing,
> Don't attach to anything.

Going, coming refers to phenomena rising and falling in your mind, whether they are of people, thoughts, ideas, feelings, or external objects. Just let go of them all. You may feel on top of the world after a good sitting and wish you could meditate forever. After a bad sitting you may want to give up meditation. Good and bad come and go, but attaching to either is vexation. If you sat well today, that's fine; now forget it. If you can't let it go, I guarantee you won't sit well tomorrow. If you did not sit well, forget that too.

For our purposes, *sitting, standing* refers to sitting practice. Some people like sitting, others prefer walking meditation. I'm sure some would prefer meditating lying down, or even in their sleep. For some, the Chan Center is a good environment, for others it is not. In the beginning of retreat, these factors influence your practice, but after a few days you should be accustomed to the environment. Let go of any ideas of what you think is best for you. When you practice, whether the environment suits your taste should not matter, nor should which method you are using. This center is set up to be conducive to practice. Take advantage of the seven days of opportunity and the lack of distractions. When you are really working hard on your method, none of these issues will bother you.

Practicing in different ways—sitting, walking, prostrating, working—trains your mind and body to do well under all conditions. It is not true that you can only reach deep levels of meditation through sitting. You can even enter samadhi while prostrating or even during walking meditation. When I ask you not to use your mind, to let your body walk on its own, it is possible to do just that. At that time, you would feel weightless, even lose your sense of body. All these methods help you lose your attachments.

4.4 ▪ Entering the Gate of Chan

> Affirming no direction,
> Can there be leaving and entering?

Leaving and entering refers to the gate of Chan, which has neither shape nor location, yet is infinitely vast. Here is a story I reserve for retreats. As a result of unwavering diligence you arrive at the gate of Chan. Before the gate stands a gatekeeper who says, "First you must put down your weapons." Being determined to pass through the gate, you give it no second thought, so you drop all your defenses. After that the guard says, "Next you must take off all your clothes." You think for a moment, and then you drop all your remaining attachments. Then the guard says, "Now you have to put aside your body." You have been working hard for a long time so you decide that enlightenment is even worth dying for, so away goes the body. Finally, the guard says, "You still have your mind; that too must go. There can be nothing left of you when you enter." Because you are determined to succeed, you agree to this final demand. The instant that you let go of your mind, the gate disappears. There was in fact no gate to pass through and nothing to enter.

Do you have this kind of determination and faith? Giving up your attachments is hard enough—you are also asked to give up your body and mind. Did you know that practicing Chan demanded so much? You may feel that being deluded is not so bad after all. At least you still exist. I have no power to force you to do anything; it's all up to you.

This metaphor of giving up everything for liberation can be frightening, but remember we are all beginners, not yet at the gate of Chan. For now all you need to do is practice. Put down your previous thought and do not cling to your next thought. Stay in the present moment until everything else falls away. Eventually and quite naturally, the present moment will not exist either. Easy, isn't it? If you have heard that we are already enlightened, but we are just not aware of it, that is a serious misconception. What you should have heard is that we are all originally buddhas, but we have not yet discovered it for ourselves. Enlightenment is this discovery. A buddha sees all sentient beings as buddhas, but sentient beings see sentient beings as just that.

Affirming no direction means that the methods taught by the Buddha all lead to the gate of Chan, but once there, to speak of "direction" has no meaning.

4.5 ▪ Get on the Bus to Buddhahood

> There is neither unifying nor dispersing,
> Neither slow nor quick.

The first line in this stanza refers to space, the second, to time. There are newlyweds here whom I have forbidden to have anything to do with each other for seven days. They may think I have separated them, but I haven't really. They are still husband and wife. If they are truly inseparable, no one can pull them apart, though nothing can bring them completely together as one entity either.

Even the organs within one's body are separate and distinct. If they were compressed into one mass, nothing would function. The ordinary mind is like this. Thoughts come and go all the time. If the mind were one, how could you feel greedy one moment, sated the next, sad one moment, and happy later? For this reason we say that the body and mind are illusory, and as long as things are illusory there is no unity.

Only true mind, or no-mind, is one. There is no separation within or outside it, therefore, there is no need to talk about space. So where is this true mind? If you say it is everywhere, then this is not true mind. Unified mind is everywhere, but no-mind has no spatial dimension—it is everywhere *and* nowhere. Thus, no-mind transcends unified mind. Unified mind recognizes only existence, so it is not ultimate awareness; no-mind goes beyond, recognizing both existence *and* nonexistence without discrimination.

Neither slow nor quick refers to the time it takes to reach enlightenment, as well as to the time after enlightenment. Many practitioners wonder if and when they will get enlightened. When some older people find out I became a monk at thirteen they become discouraged, thinking they won't have enough time to reach enlightenment. Nonsense. Remember, enlightenment can come in an instant. Is there a queue at the gate of Chan? Are you only allowed in one at a time? You don't have to take a number and wait in line to achieve buddhahood. Do buddhas have seniority over others? Do buddhas compare notes on when and how they got enlightened? Funny as it sounds, some people go through similar mental maneuvers. "That person over there sits like a rock; she must nearly be enlightened. I've been on twenty retreats, so I must be closer to enlightenment than that guy, who is on his first one." Do these thoughts sound familiar?

It is never too late to start practicing. If you missed the first bus to buddhahood, the next one will be by soon. The important thing is to get on the bus and stay on. Once you accept Buddhadharma and begin to practice, continue doing so. Being vexed, getting lost in wandering thoughts, and having attachments do not necessarily mean you are getting off the bus. Such obstructions are part of practice and will be with you all your life. Practice is precisely recognizing these obstructions and persevering nevertheless. The most serious obstacle of all is to anticipate enlightenment. Expectations like that will sap one's strength.

When you reach buddhahood, there is no space or time, no separation between self and others, between past and future. After enlightenment there are no longer attachments. Ordinarily we are self-centered and do things primarily for our own benefit. After enlightenment, we do things to benefit others. Of course, I am talking about complete enlightenment. The initial enlightenment experience just means you have seen into the nature of non-self. It is a flash of realization. Afterward, one is still not yet a buddha, just a sentient being with vexations and attachments. However, the power from that experience can fuel a much deeper and stronger practice. How long the power lasts depends on your diligence. Practice does not end after enlightenment. In fact, one should practice doubly hard after an enlightenment experience. If it sounds like all I talk about is practice, you are right. That is why we are here—to practice.

Brightness and tranquillity
are just as they are

5.1 ▓ Allow the Mind to Float and Sink

> Brightness and tranquillity are just as
>   they are.
> They cannot be explained in words.
>
> Mind is without alienation;
> No need to terminate lust.

Brightness refers to wisdom, *tranquillity* refers to the absence of vexation. *Just as they are* means that brightness and tranquillity are present whether one practices or not, since practicing does not create wisdom. The *Platform Sutra* says, "deluded, it is vexation; awakened, it is bodhi." Bodhi is never apart from vexation. Because they are deluded, sentient beings ordinarily perceive that vexation and bodhi are separate, but buddhas understand that vexation and wisdom are identical. There is no such thing as an enlightened being "cutting off vexation."

Thus, the *Song* says, *No need to terminate lust*, meaning vexation. If you came here with goals and expectations, I can save you some time: the enlightenment you seek does not exist. Knowing this should be a heavy burden off your back. Now you can relax and put all your effort into practice without thoughts of gain or loss. The *Song* says that wisdom and vexation are one and the same, so what is there to gain or lose?

Learning that there is nothing to gain, you may question why you should even practice and attend retreats. The point is that if you have expectations, you will create more vexations, so just relax. Do not fear wandering thoughts, vexations, or changing physical and mental conditions. If you must fear something, let it be the mind of seeking and aversion.

There is no need to press or berate yourself when you feel exhausted. It doesn't mean you are weak or a failure. When you are depleted of energy and your mind is completely scattered, relax. Sit on the cushion and rest. Don't even bother with the method. Allow your body and mind to rejuvenate. Forcing would only tire you more and create frustration. If you do not want to rest, you can get up and do slow prostration. That will gently settle the mind and the movement will help to revive you from your physical torpor.

> Nature being empty, lust will depart by itself.
> Allow the mind to float and sink.

> Neither clear nor clouded,
> Neither shallow nor deep.

The first line might be better understood as: "Since the nature of dharmas is emptiness, one naturally departs from vexation." Dharmas, or phenomena, are inherently empty—they are not enduring and have no independent existence. Realizing the inherent emptiness of dharmas, there is no need to either seek or avoid them. When there is no attachment there is also no vexation. Hence, when one understands that dharmas are empty, vexations will depart by themselves.

Dealing with vexations by suppressing, opposing, or attaching to them only creates further vexations and obstructions. I tell practitioners to ignore their wandering thoughts, but they sometimes mistake this to mean repressing or blocking them. Actually, it means acknowledging wandering thoughts but not attaching to them. Let them come, let them go. As the *Song* says, *Allow the mind to float and sink.*

Allowing the mind to float and sink is a sure sign of progress. To the enlightened, wandering thoughts are no longer vexations. If you saw a Chan master scolding students and disciples, would that be a vexation for the master? By the end of this retreat you may get that opportunity.

People usually consider anger to be a vexation. Yet, there have been numerous accounts of angry masters and patriarchs. Once, Manjusri Bodhisattva held a sword to the Buddha and said, "What kind of buddha are you? It seems you have come to *bring* vexations to people. It might be better that I kill you."

To fully enlightened beings, vexation is wisdom and wisdom is vexation. Therefore, anger becomes a response whose source is wisdom. Buddhas respond to the needs of sentient beings. If anger is needed, buddhas will show anger, after which they simply move on to the next moment. Attaching to anger may lead us to do or say harmful things, and even affect us physically. When bad fortune befalls enlightened beings, they do not suffer from it. And good fortune is no different, since to these beings, all dharmas are empty. Ordinary people cannot deal with the world and their lives in this manner. For them to pretend to be unaffected by good or bad fortune only creates more vexations.

The mind of an enlightened person is perceived as clear and deep, while ordinary mind is perceived as cloudy and shallow. But to the enlightened there is no difference between clear and cloudy, deep and shallow. Again, we cannot pretend that our cloudy, shallow minds are in fact deep and clear. We practice because we understand that our mind is cloudy, scattered, and confused. Otherwise, we wouldn't bother meditating. Experienced practitioners also know that with practice, the mind clarifies and becomes more insightful.

There are three levels of clarity. First is the ordinary clarity one can cultivate through meditation. By retreat's end, most of you will have experienced such clarity. The second level stems from samadhi and is a profound clarity. The third level comes with enlightenment, where clarity naturally and spontaneously arises in any and all situations.

When you meditate consistently over a long time, your *chi* (energy or life force) will flow smoothly with few obstructions, and the mind will be much clearer and brighter. However, we should not seek such results. If they happen, they just come naturally as side benefits. Nor do we focus on cultivating samadhi. The goal is simply to collect the scattered mind, unify it, and then go beyond that to experience no-mind. Not that samadhi is bad; it will at least temporarily reduce our vexations and clarify our minds. For some however, the bliss of samadhi can become an attachment and a pitfall.

There is shallow enlightenment and there is complete enlightenment. Shallow enlightenment (seeing into one's self-nature) is similar to samadhi in that its benefits are temporary. On the other hand, complete enlightenment cuts off vexations forever. To the greatly enlightened, there is neither vexation nor wisdom. Wisdom only exists for those who have vexations.

Here and now most of you are practicing concentration at the level of focusing the mind. Once you collect the mind you can begin practicing Chan. If you continue to practice you will gradually understand the nature of clarity and confusion, wisdom and vexation.

5.2 ▨ Original Mind Is Right Now

> Originally it was not ancient;
> At present it is not modern.
>
> Now it is non-abiding;
> Now it is original mind.
> Originally it did not exist;
> "Origin" is the present moment.

One of you asked, "If originally Buddha and vexations are one, how did sentient beings come about?" Relatively speaking, there are such things as beginnings and ends. People have birth dates and death dates. That is clear. Ultimately speaking however, there are no beginnings. If you were able to travel in a straight line, you would ultimately cross your point of origin. Physicists believe that the universe is curved as well, and there is speculation that the same may be true for time. In fact, time and space are interdependent. Without space one would have no way of perceiving time, and without time there would be no way of perceiving space.

It is difficult to grasp the idea of a circular time-space continuum without a beginning. Our perceptions and range of experience are extremely limited. It would seem pointless to go anywhere if we only ended up in the same place. In fact, that rarely happens. Most people take detours, get lost, forget where they are, stop, turn back, spin in circles. Walking forward until you come full circle, however, is a worthwhile experience. On your journey, you are bound to discover, learn, and enjoy interesting things that you would otherwise not experience.

Walking in a straight line until you cross your starting point is a metaphor for Chan practice. You begin with a mind of vexation and end up with a mind of wisdom, but as I said before, vexation and wisdom are the same. You are still "you," yet "you" have changed. You begin at square one as a confused sentient being, and when you are enlightened you find yourself back on square one. You are the same person, but your perception has changed.

In the phrase *Originally it was not ancient*, "it" refers to the original mind. In essence, it means that the original mind is not something that once was but is no longer. Original mind is your mind right now, without beginning or end. *At present it is not modern* means that you do not make wisdom out of vexation; one does not grow out of the ashes of the other.

Time does not apply to enlightenment and original mind. Is your face today old or new? Was your face at the age of one old or new? These are meaningless questions, yet it is ingrained in our minds to view everything as a continuum from past to present to future. Original mind is always old, always new, and always present.

There is a practitioner here whose wife is pregnant. I have some questions for him: "Is your love for her different now that she is pregnant? Do you love her more or less? Does it mean you have different minds, one that used to be half-filled with love, and a new one that is completely filled?" From our usual point of view, it may appear that there are different minds for different situations, places, and times. The mind of vexation has innumerable faces. But the mind that the *Song of Mind* speaks of is original mind, a pure mind without vexations. This mind does not change.

When you awaken and vexation becomes wisdom, you will understand that the past mind is no different from the present mind. Therefore, there is no need to resent your mind of vexation. Simply practice hard, and quite naturally this mind of vexation will become the mind of wisdom. Upon realizing enlightenment, Chan Master Hanshan (1546–1623)—not to be confused with Hanshan, the Tang dynasty poet—said that he now knew that his nostrils pointed downward. Prior to this he was not an idiot; he just came full circle, from knowing his nostrils pointed downward with the mind of vexation, to knowing it with the mind of wisdom. There is no Pure Land apart from this world to strive for. Phenomena themselves are the truth.

Now it is non-abiding; now it is original mind. The *Diamond Sutra* admonishes us to give rise to the mind without any attachment. Grasping at nothing, original mind is unfettered by the external environment. This is the non-abiding mind. When you practice, ask yourself, "Does my mind abide anywhere?" If it does, it is a mind of vexation. Do not be disappointed; this is where we must begin: we try to collect the scattered mind and make it simple and focused. To attain non-abiding, we must first attain a mind that abides on one point.

When the mind is scattered it abides in many places, hopping from here to there, clinging to one thing, getting confused by another. This is the mind we bring to the cushion. We practice to collect the mind, to train it to abide on one thing, the method.

If while meditating you constantly shift, scratch, sigh, or do any number of things, where does your mind abide? It is being pulled by your physical condition and thoughts. Practice is gradually training the mind to abide where you want it to abide.

Originally, it did not exist. "Origin" is the present moment. Original mind has no origin; it is this mind at this moment. Some people have the power to read other people's pasts and futures. However, they must do so by entering the minds of the other people. So where is original mind? Is it the mind they see in the past or the mind they see in the future? It is neither. It is the mind at this moment.

Since the mind of the Buddha abides nowhere, it does not exist. Minds exist only when they abide in something. Practice to have your mind abide where you want it to; don't let it scamper about. Here on retreat life is simple. Put your mind on the method. The rest will take care of itself.

5.3 ▩ Stalking a Wild Rabbit

> Bodhi has always existed;
> No need to preserve it.
> Vexation has never existed;
> No need to eliminate it.

First, Niutou says that original mind originally did not exist. One stanza later he says that bodhi has always existed, and that vexation has never existed. Despite sounding contradictory, Niutou is saying something important. That bodhi has always existed gives us the faith and courage to cultivate ourselves and work toward an attainable goal. That vexation has never existed helps to release us from its clutches; we need not feel compelled or resigned to indulge in it.

Some people think there is no bodhi to attain, while others fear that after attaining bodhi, they will lose it. In the *Platform Sutra*, Huineng (638–713) relates a poem submitted to Fifth Patriarch Hongren (602–675) by a monk named Shenxiu (d. 702).

> Our body is the bodhi tree
> And our mind a mirror bright.
> Carefully we wipe them hour by hour,
> and let no dust alight.

This reflects the attitude of wanting to maintain bodhi mind so that vexations will not come up. While there is no need to worry that bodhi will be defiled, this doesn't mean that practice is pointless. Remember, the *Song* speaks from the enlightened point of view. In order for us to realize these truths, we must practice. If we do not, we will never know that bodhi is always present and that vexation does not exist.

> Natural wisdom is self-illuminating;
> All dharmas return to thusness.
> There is no returning, no receiving;
> Stop contemplating, forget keeping.

Natural wisdom refers to original mind and has always existed. It is self-illuminating and has never known vexation. If buddha-nature can be defiled by vexation, it would not be buddha-nature. Natural wisdom is always present and has never been lost. Our delusion keeps us from seeing it. As an analogy, we may say that the clouds are blocking the sun, but that really isn't so. Nothing is blocking the sun. It is our limited point of view on earth that makes it seem as such. In order to see the sun for what it really is we would have to be the sun. Realizing one's true nature is like seeing the sun with the clouds parted. This does not make one a buddha, but at least one has seen one's self-nature. It is not the same as seeing the whole sun; the atmosphere still obscures the sun's true nature. But the sun itself is not bothered by clouds or the atmosphere, just as buddha-nature is not troubled by vexation.

All dharmas return to thusness means that all phenomena (dharmas), whether material or mental, ceaselessly change and move. Nevertheless the *Song* says that they are in reality, "thus." Originally there are no differences between them; their seeming differences are illusory just as the sun that you see is an illusion. To us, dharmas constantly change, but when original wisdom appears, we realize that all dharmas *return to thusness*. The term "return," however, can be misleading. There is no place to which dharmas return. It is not as if there is a giant warehouse that receives dharmas. This is the meaning of *There is no returning, no receiving*. It clears up the idea that there might be something like a god to which all things return.

Stop contemplating, forget keeping speaks of a method of practice. Because original wisdom is forever illuminating, one should not need to practice. This must seem strange, especially to those who have spent so much time and energy meditating. If you feel these words apply to you, then you may as well go home. The observation is from the standpoint of one who has given rise to natural wisdom. But since we have not yet realized this, we must practice. "Contemplating" means engaging your method; "keeping" means not letting it slip away.

Working on the method is like stalking a wild rabbit; you must be patient and careful. If the rabbit senses you, it will flee. If you realize you are sitting well and you think, "I'm sitting very well," it's like announcing yourself to the rabbit. If you are clear and focused, the method will leave you as soon as you congratulate yourself. Similarly, when you become aware that your legs and back do not hurt anymore, the pain returns. We have yet to reveal our natural wisdom, so we are not ready to talk about the "thusness" of dharmas, let alone stopping contemplation. We accept where we are and work from there.

5.4 ■ The Four Virtues

> The four virtues are unborn;
> The three bodies have always existed.
> The six sense organs contact their realms;
> Discrimination is not consciousness.

The *four virtues* refer to aspects of nirvana: permanence, joy, self, and purity. The *three bodies* are the three transcendent bodies (*trikaya*) of the Buddha: the *dharmakaya*, the *sambhogakaya*, and the *nirmanakaya*. The *six sense organs* are the eye, the ear, the nose, the tongue, the body, and the mind. Consciousness beyond discrimination is the enlightenment experience, the mind that has opened up and brightened.

The four virtues of nirvana seem identical to what Buddhism considers to be the illusory views of ordinary sentient beings. Is this a contradiction? First, we must investigate what Buddhism says about the delusory thinking of people. Buddhism speaks of the four marks of samsaric existence: impermanence, suffering, no-self, and impurity. These are the opposites of the four virtues of nirvana.

First, all things are impermanent—they arise, come together, break up, and vanish due to causes and conditions. Nothing has permanence or independence; therefore, nothing has self-nature. Suffering arises because of causes and conditions. This is so because our bodies and minds are impure, defiled.

Would you say that your life is total joy? I doubt it, just as I would doubt it if you said your life were total suffering. Buddhism's idea of suffering is intimately associated with the concept of impermanence. Buddhism also recognizes the experience of joy. Without joy, human existence would not continue. It is only because we have experienced joy that we search for more. For some, their desires are also a kind of joy. One might say that life is the pursuit of joy, but to say that we experience nothing but joy would be incorrect.

In fact, we experience both suffering and joy. If there were only joy, Shakyamuni Buddha would never have felt the need to practice. Then what is this joy that we feel? Our joy is what we experience in the transient realm of desire. It is not the true joy of nirvana. Those who are attached to worldly joys are unable even to experience samadhi, let alone enlightenment.

Those who have a deep connection with suffering do better in practice. One needs a certain amount of determination in one's practice. People whose life is joyful all the time may not exert themselves, whereas those who suffer a lot might practice in order to escape samsara. This is the way of the arhat. The way for the bodhisattva is to vow to help sentient beings end *their* suffering. Thus, having a deep understanding of the suffering nature of life is essential to Mahayana practice.

When we perform our daily morning and evening services, we repeat the vow to deliver innumerable sentient beings. How many of you understand the depth of what you are saying? Perhaps you are just reciting it without having a deep conviction of wanting to help sentient beings. It's not that you don't care. I'm sure all of us care about others to some extent. It's just that we don't really feel that much suffering. We feel that our own lives are not so bad and that people around us are also doing quite well. Since we don't have a strong sense of suffering, we do not have a strong desire to deliver sentient beings. In fact, if you went around trying to help deliver others, some would undoubtedly ask you to mind your own business. Only when you really know that suffering is inherent to life will you have genuine concern for sentient beings.

Do chickens, cows, and pigs suffer? I'm sure some people don't think about it at all, and simply believe that these animals are meant to be food for us. What if we were cattle waiting to be slaughtered? That would be suffering. We are not in that situation...or are we? On the other hand, maybe cows, chickens, and pigs don't suffer. Maybe they aren't aware that they are to be slaughtered. Maybe they feel they have pretty good lives.

They get unlimited food, they're taken care of, have some room to roam. It's a good life, while it lasts.

I use this analogy because like these animals, many people do not even realize that they are suffering. We fight with each other and with ourselves; we don't have control of the world, our bodies, our minds or emotions. We are vexed all the time, but when asked, we may say that life is pretty good. In this sense we aren't much different from the domestic animals we feed and then slaughter. This is pitiful.

Suffering stems from impermanence and impurity. Even joy eventually becomes suffering because it doesn't last. Eventually we lose what we love; we get sick; we die. The four virtues of permanence, joy, self, and purity refer to nirvana, wisdom, and buddha-nature. These things have no beginning or end, so of course they are permanent. Nirvana does not start when a person attains buddhahood; it has always been without beginning. The same is true for buddha-nature; it is not because you practice that buddha-nature begins—it has always existed. The same is true for natural wisdom. These things are truly permanent. Permanence cannot grow out of impermanence; the truly permanent has always been permanent.

Again, true joy does not come and go; it is uninterrupted and permanent. Every evening I ask you, "Has today been a good day?" Some say yes, some say no, some remain silent. For the people who say yes, was it truly a good day? To truly have a good day, you must have an understanding of what a good day is. You would have to experience good days all the time. All days must be equally good. If you say that today is a good day, but yesterday wasn't, then today wasn't truly good either. It's good only in comparison to the previous day. Tomorrow may be better. Does that mean that today wasn't quite as good as you thought it was? If you were to say that all your days have been good, and then leave this retreat and get hit by a truck, would you stick to your word and say, "Ah, today's a good day"?

All the joys that we experience, whether physical, mental, or emotional, derive from the realm of desire. They are temporary. Therefore, they cannot be considered true joys. Heavenly beings experience bliss because they are not constrained by bodies as we are. However, their joy is also limited and temporary. People in samadhi experience dhyana joy —they transcend body, space, and time—but samadhi eventually fades too, and people who have experienced dhyana joy want to meditate to regain that great joy. Unfortunately, it too is limited and impermanent.

Also, regardless of what kind of joy one experiences, it always seems short in comparison to the experience of suffering. This is to be understood from our subjective point of view. I'll give a couple of examples. A sleep that is comfortable, peaceful, and relaxed seems to pass quickly. Nightmares, on the other hand, seem to drag on forever. If you are meditating well, time flies. But if your legs hurt it takes forever for that bell to ring. Objectively time might be the same, but from our subjective point of view suffering lingers and joy is fleeting.

The self that we experience in ordinary life is not the true self. It is an illusion, based on imagination and vexations. Reflect on this: What is the self? It is the stringing together of many illusions and thoughts. We speak of the self as something that belongs to "me," something that's "mine," or something that "I am." But the self is only a series of consecutive thoughts—the previous thought generating a subsequent thought—all of which create the illusion of a self. Only an illusory mind can derive from vexations that in turn come from fundamental ignorance. And fundamental ignorance has no beginning.

Our thoughts are constantly changing. Where in this turbulence is there a self? It is only buddha-nature, nirvana, and wisdom that never change. Only these are the true self. The ordinary self that we know is an illusion.

Something that is truly pure never changes, but fundamentally there is no "pure" or "impure." These are distinctions we make because of our confusion and discrimination. But there can never be true purity while there is discrimination, and discrimination comes from the mind of illusion and vexation.

The true states of permanence, joy, self, and purity are aspects of nirvana; however, if when you enter nirvana there are still four virtues, then it is really attachment, and you have not entered it. These so-called four virtues are only goals that lead us toward nirvana. Upon entering nirvana, there is no discrimination left, and therefore no need to speak of the four virtues.

The *three bodies* refers to the *trikaya*, or the transcendent bodies of the Buddha, which exist as distinct entities only to sentient beings. The *dharmakaya*, the body of essential nature, is that which is universal and unmoving. This aspect of the Buddha does not exist in any particular location, shape, or form. It is ubiquitous, universally existent.

The *sambhogakaya* can be understood as the "reward" or "enjoyment" body. It is that aspect that exists in the Pure Land of the buddhas and is perceived only by buddhas. There can be sentient beings in this Pure Land, but the Pure Land they perceive will not be the same as that which the buddhas perceive. Only bodhisattvas above the first *bhumi* (stage of the bodhisattva path) will be able to perceive the *sambhogakaya* of a particular buddha, but even so, it will be their own perception, not that of the buddha.

We may think we all see the same Chan Hall, but in fact, everybody sees something different. Some of you think there are ghosts here. Perhaps what you see as ghosts I see as buddhas, bodhisattvas, and arhats. Because we have different mental states we see different things; so even if people reside in the Pure Land of a particular buddha, they do not see what that buddha sees.

As a matter of fact, I do see ghosts in this Chan Hall, but they are not the ghosts you might be thinking of. One participant said she saw the ghosts of dead people. What I see are the ghosts of all of you here. You have spent your entire lives with ghosts. You deal with the ghosts of your habits, preconceptions, vexations, greed, anger, arrogance, and doubt. Your ghosts are with you now, even as you listen to this lecture, even as you meditate.

The *nirmanakaya*, also known as the "transformation" or "incarnation" body of the Buddha, is that aspect of the Buddha which delivers sentient beings, and appears anytime and anywhere to do so. The *nirmanakaya* can come in two forms. The incarnation body comes to the world through human birth, as in the case of Shakyamuni Buddha. The transformation body can appear in the form of a buddha, but also in any other guise. Whatever helps you in your practice and life should be recognized as the *nirmanakaya* of a buddha.

Without consciously or intentionally doing so, someone may actually help you on the practice path. At that time and in that sense, that person would be the *nirmanakaya* of a buddha. The help may be noticeably positive or it may seem to be negative or hurtful; but if it directs you further in the practice of the Dharma, it is the help of the *nirmanakaya*. As practitioners we should consider all sentient beings as the *nirmanakayas* of innumerable buddhas. It could be a friend, stranger, or adversary; a spider, fly, or rat. Everybody, everything, is the *nirmanakaya* of a buddha.

> The six sense organs contact their realms;
> Discrimination is not consciousness.

These lines refer to those beings who have already revealed their buddha-minds. Such people still have full use of their six senses, but these senses are no longer controlled by ordinary consciousness; rather, they are functions of wisdom. Ordinary consciousness is emotional and involves attachment. Wisdom derives from nonattachment. At another time, I spoke of fundamental wisdom and acquired wisdom. They can be understood like this: *fundamental wisdom* arises when one is enlightened; using this wisdom through the six sense organs is *acquired wisdom*.

Here we are speaking of bodhisattvas and buddhas. However, ordinary sentient beings are different. Whatever phenomena arise while we are meditating is illusory. One of you, while meditating today, thought you saw and caught a rabbit. Some of you are also disturbed by the flies that have found their way into the Chan Hall. Obviously there are no rabbits in this building, but from a practitioner's point of view, you should see all phenomena, including rabbits and flies, as illusory.

While meditating do not allow your mind to interact with these external phenomena. Your mind should be undisturbed by whatever happens. Regard everything as illusion. Think of yourself as a Buddha statue. Is a statue disturbed by flies? Turn your body into a statue and work with your moving mind.

The six senses of the enlightened still respond to the environment, but these individuals are disturbed by nothing, whether an annoying fly or beautiful music. We are not at this level yet. To cultivate yourselves, stay on your method and disregard whatever is happening. Next, no matter what is happening to you, treat it as having nothing to do with you. We do not have to be enlightened to emulate this attitude. Daily life is different. Whatever you are doing, wherever your hands are, that is where your mind should be. This is being mindful and is good practice. You may not become enlightened overnight, but you will be on a good path.

In one-mindedness there are no wandering thoughts

6.1 ■ Practice Is Also a Wandering Thought

> In one-mindedness there are no wandering
>   thoughts,
> The myriad conditions harmonize.

All vexations of body and mind are wandering thoughts. Today some-one recited a line from the *Diamond Sutra*, "Not abiding, the mind arises," and asked if it meant having no motivation, or doing nothing. Actually, the line describes the state after enlightenment when wisdom arises and the mind is not attached to anything. When you have motivated your-self to meditate, the will to practice is still a wandering thought. When we are practicing hard, we are still using this false mind (wandering thoughts). On the other hand, true mind is no-mind. How can one practice if there is no-mind?

Everything you do, including meditation, falls under false mind, but if you don't use this false mind to practice, you will never arrive at true mind. The progression of practice is from scattered mind to concen-trated mind, from that to unified mind, and from one-mind to no-mind. The first three stages—scattered, concentrated, and unified mind—are all illusory. Only rarely can someone realize no-mind without first going through these three stages.

Right now, most of you are going from scattered mind to concen-trated mind. Experiencing success even at this level is good practice. Perhaps you will only experience concentrated mind fleetingly during this retreat. If you spend the entire retreat thinking about your daily life, then you will have remained with your scattered mind. For these reasons we need methods that lead a scattered mind to concentrated mind, to unified mind, and beyond.

People often think they got enlightened when all they experienced was unified mind. They might describe the experience as joyful and liberating, but discrimination still exists. There are even different levels of unification. The first is unification of body and mind, the second, of self and environment, while the third is universal, unlimited unification.

Some of you may have already tasted the first level of unification. If you have forgotten yourselves and are no longer aware of your body and thoughts, that is good. By the time you reach the second level, your joy will be greater because you will not be discriminating between self and others. Boundless unification is profound and can only be reached in deep samadhi. Such people may feel they have no more vexations, but subtle discriminations still persist.

In no-mind, one feels there is nothing that needs to be done, yet one still does things. This brings us back to the *Diamond Sutra*, which says, "not abiding, the mind arises." One is not attached to one's own existence or that of others, yet one still interacts with and helps others. Outwardly such a person seems like any other.

The term "one-mind" may be misleading here, since it does not refer to unified mind, but to no-mind—the same true mind experienced by all buddhas. It is important to distinguish between the one-mind of ordinary people (unified mind) and the one-mind of the buddhas (no-mind/true mind).

The phrase *myriad conditions harmonize* should not be confused with the joy of experiencing one-mind. If such a state is perceived as harmonious and beautiful, that is still an attachment. This is good, but it is not no-mind. The one-mind of the buddhas perceives that all dharmas are just as they are. There is no addition of "this is beautiful" or "this is peaceful."

You may wonder what would be the point of enlightenment if things are not seen as beautiful and peaceful. The point is that these are aspects of illusory mind, and are as illusory as ugliness and violence. What would buddhas do if they came upon a violent battle? Obviously their own welfare is of little concern to them. Would they see that others are suffering injury? The answer is both no and yes. On the one hand, they see dharmas, or phenomena, as they are, and so the battle is just as it is. On the other hand, they will perceive that sentient beings see it as suffering, and so will do their part to help in any way they can.

"What Is This?"

> Mind and nature are intrinsically equal;
> Together, yet one does not necessarily lead
>   to the other.

Mind is the buddha-mind that functions from wisdom. *Nature* refers to the essential buddha-nature of all dharmas as they are, without our added discrimination. When the mind is clear of vexations one can see the buddha-nature of all dharmas. The minds of ordinary people function from discrimination and vexation, so they cannot perceive the buddha-nature that is inherent in everything. We tend to perceive things in relation to other things: this is better, that is worse, I am smarter, you are more beautiful, and so on. With this kind of discriminating mind, one cannot experience the buddha-mind.

I once held the incense board in front of a practitioner and asked, "What is this?" He grabbed the other end of the board and said, "This is this." That is nondiscrimination. It didn't matter that it was a piece of wood, it could have been an animal, another person, or love. At that moment, there was no discrimination in his mind, so he could have said or done anything. His particular words and actions weren't important.

A famous gong'an illustrates this: Chan master Baizhang (720–814) held up his favorite vase in front of his head monk and another monk named Weishan, who at that time was the cook. Baizhang said, "You can't call it a vase. Now tell me what is it?"

The head monk answered, "Well, you cannot call it a block of wood." By this he meant that if one cannot call it a vase, then one also cannot call it something else.

Baizhang then asked Weishan the same question. Weishan kicked the vase and broke it, and when Baizhang asked again, Weishan ran out of the room without answering. Answering would have been too much, but if he hadn't kicked it over it would have seemed as if he hadn't addressed the question at all.

The head monk remained behind, waiting and wondering what had happened, and whether he had answered correctly. Baizhang looked at him and said, "He knows, you don't." The point is that the head monk wanted to know what had happened, and whether his answer was correct, whereas Weishan had nothing in his mind, including ideas of right or wrong, winning or losing.

For the average person, a vase is a vase; it has its form and function. When a person points out that a vase is a vase, he or she is using the mind of discrimination. If the disciple had turned the situation around and asked Master Baizhang the same question, how do you think the master would have replied? If Baizhang had said, "It's a vase," he would have been correct. If the disciple had also said, "It's a vase," he too may have been correct. However, Baizhang had already eliminated that option because he wanted to see if there was any attachment—or anything at all—in the minds of his disciples. The mind of attachment views things in a limited way. The mind of nonattachment sees everything as equal. To truly see everything as equal is to see buddha-nature, because mind and nature are intrinsically equal.

Together, yet one does not necessarily lead to the other refers to the difference between mind and nature. The one-mind of the Buddha sees all dharmas as equal; the mind of vexation sees everything with discrimination. However, the essential nature of both mind and nature is the same and equal. It is because of this that we can realize intrinsic mind. After a day of meditating, do you have minds of equality or are you still discriminating?

When we are practicing hard we are using wandering thoughts, which is precisely the mind of vexation. Only when there is no longer any way to continue using wandering thoughts will wisdom arise. We use methods of concentration to unify the mind. After the mind and body are unified, we switch to a *huatou* to break apart the unified mind. We need to go beyond unified mind in order to experience the wisdom that arises when there is no attachment.

I hope you can use this retreat to move from scattered mind to concentrated mind and eventually to unified mind. The best way to concentrate the mind is to not be afraid of wandering thoughts. Staying with the method is all that is necessary. Don't analyze how well or badly you think you may be doing. That is a sure sign that you are off the method.

6.2 ▪ According with Phenomena

> Without arising, complying with
>   phenomena,
> Abiding hidden everywhere.

The term "non-arising" is ever present in Buddhist texts. It means no thought, no attachment, no vexation, no defilement. Nothing vexes completely enlightened practitioners. They comply with all phenomena, recognizing different dharmas without interfering with them.

Previously I asked how you thought buddhas would react in the face of war and carnage. *Complying with phenomena* means that enlightened beings would still react normally to a given situation even though they themselves are unaffected by it. Therefore, buddhas would comply with phenomena and act accordingly; they would not be unresponsive to violence and war. Furthermore, it is possible for unenlightened practitioners to see someone die and not view it as someone dying, or witness a house on fire, and not view it as something burning.

A lay practitioner whose house was robbed told his upset wife, "It doesn't matter, the thief didn't steal anything of ours. He really stole his own belongings." When the thief heard what the husband said, he figured that the man was an idiot and returned to take his wife. The wife asked, "Now what are you going to do?"

The husband replied, "No matter, he's just taking his own wife. It has nothing to do with me." This person thought he was not discriminating between what belonged to him and what belonged to others. Is this the kind of nondiscriminating mind you look forward to achieving?

One of my students had a suitcase of jewelry stolen by some boys, yet continued to believe they were sweet and innocent. After a retreat another student gave away all of his money and possessions to friends and strangers. Those belongings that he felt were not worth giving away, he threw away. His close friends wanted him to go to a mental hospital for observation, but he protested that it was others who were crazy.

These anecdotes show us that situations like these are not limited to stories from long ago. They happen today to people like you and me. More important, I want to stress that this is *not* what the sutras and texts mean when they speak of "non-arising" and of "complying with phenomena." I am not saying these three people acted irrationally, only that they are not enlightened, and were not "complying with phenomena." There are numerous mental states that may arise in the course of practice, so what these practitioners experienced is unclear. Perhaps their actions were deluded, or perhaps they were experiencing an intermediate level of practice.

What is meant by *Abiding hidden everywhere?* The person who has achieved the level of *complying with phenomena* need not stay secluded in the mountains or hide away somewhere. He or she can be anywhere—in the midst of quietude or activity—and be perfectly fine. In a sense, you take the peace of secluded practice everywhere you go. Therefore, you can abide in all places equally. You do not have to reach a profound level of practice to achieve this quietude. Some of you may be experiencing a degree of it right now. On the first day of retreat most of you were disturbed by the sounds in the street, but as time passes, you will be less and less disturbed by these phenomena. Of course this is not samadhi, for if it were, you wouldn't hear anything at all. However, if you acknowledge the sounds around you without reacting to them, and just continue with your method, that is already good practice.

In the course of practice most of you will experience unification with the external environment. On the other hand, I am fairly sure that most of you will not give away all of your possessions. This is not to say that the people I described earlier were crazy, but things like that don't happen very often. There is a stage of practice described as "seeing that mountains are not mountains and rivers are not rivers." This is a normal stage in one's practice, but everyone acts differently. Most people who experience this level of practice do not act strangely.

At the end of retreats I tell everyone to go on with their lives as usual. It would be foolish to think that you are different from other people just because you practice. Retreats don't give you license or justification to behave differently. If it happens, it happens, but it is incorrect to act differently for the sake of being unique. If you don't want trouble, I suggest that you continue to treat your spouses and partners with respect and love and not tell them that their existence doesn't matter.

Chan is for everyone—you don't need to be a certain type of person, or lead a certain kind of life. You don't have to live in the mountains; you can practice anywhere. Throughout Buddhist history many masters, including Huineng and Niutou Farong, have said this.

Enlightenment Is Also a Wandering Thought

> Enlightenment arises from non-
> enlightenment.
> Enlightenment is non-enlightenment.

Enlightenment exists only because there are sentient beings who are not enlightened. If you attain enlightenment, is there still enlightenment? For you, no, for others, yes. Therefore, the unenlightened should pursue enlightenment. However, the enlightenment that the unenlightened pursue is an illusion, a wandering thought, and a false thought. Once you attain enlightenment, the realm of enlightenment no longer exists.

When people ask me how many levels of heaven there are, I reply that heaven, like life, is different for each person. This retreat is different for each person. Your experiences have nothing to do with anyone else's. You are in your retreat; they are in theirs. The Shifu you see is different from the Shifu others see.

Even for people born under similar circumstances, life is different. There is a saying in a Buddhist sutra that fish experience water as a palace, hungry ghosts experience it as foul-smelling pus, and human beings experience it as water. Likewise, people experience different levels of enlightenment. One great Chan master of the past described himself as having had thirty-six significant enlightenment experiences and innumerable smaller ones.

Perhaps all this talk of different kinds of enlightenment is confusing. You might think that small enlightenment is like clouds parting to reveal a star, medium enlightenment reveals the moon, and great enlightenment reveals the sun. This is not the case. Using this analogy to describe enlightenment as degrees of brightness is too limiting.

How did this master experience so many enlightenments, one after another? And why were some significant while others were small? During an enlightenment experience there are no vexations, but vexations will return when the power of the experience fades. How quickly they return of course depends on how strong these vexations were to begin with. However, when the Buddha experienced great and complete enlightenment, his vexations were forever eradicated. Nevertheless, the nature of our enlightenment is the same as the Buddha's. It is just that ours is not as deep and expansive.

However, this is a retreat, and enlightenment should not be in your thoughts. Keep only the method. Enlightenment, like street noise, has nothing to do with you. For now, both are wandering thoughts.

6.3 ▪ All Dharmas Are One Dharma

> As to gain and loss,
> Why call either good or bad?
> Everything that is active
> Originally was not created.

What is the *gain and loss* that the *Song* speaks of? Does one gain vexations and lose wisdom? Does one gain wisdom and lose vexations? I'm sure everyone would prefer the latter. Actually, both possibilities are perspectives of ordinary sentient beings. Practitioners often ask, "If everyone is originally a buddha, when did we lose wisdom and gain vexations to become ordinary sentient beings?" In fact, wisdom and vexation are always together and cannot be separated. When you gain wisdom, you gain vexation. When you gain vexation, you gain wisdom. Confusing? Let me add that if you let go of wisdom, you also let go of vexation, and if you let go of vexation, you let go of wisdom.

Wisdom itself is vexation. The wisdom of a bodhisattva is vexation as far as sentient beings are concerned; they cannot see it any other way. However, a bodhisattva does not see the vexation of sentient beings as different from wisdom. From the Buddha's point of view, there is neither wisdom nor vexation. Because you are not yet a buddha, you cannot understand this. If you are not a bodhisattva, you cannot even fathom wisdom. All you know is vexation.

Whenever you differentiate between things such as gain and loss, it leads to separation, extremes, polarities, comparisons, and judgment. As long as we are unenlightened, this is all we can do. For us there is still gain and loss, wisdom and vexation. Many come to retreat with hopes of gaining something. I'm sure some of you wondered, "What will I get out of this retreat? I'm willing to practice hard, to pay a high price, as long as there is some pay-off, something of value that I can take home." I recommend that you take a different view. As far as I'm concerned, your retreat can be considered successful if you leave with less than you brought. It would be sad if you arrived with one load of baggage and left with two. What a heavy burden! In that case I would say the Chan retreat was not worth your time and effort. On Chan retreats, the more you lose the better.

The best is to let go of so much that there will be nothing left to lose. At that time, have you gained anything? If everything is lost, how is anything gained? If you let go of even the self, what still belongs to you? I ask these loaded questions, but I hope none of you are adding this to your baggage. When we refer to the "self" or to the "I," what we mean is attachment to the self. When self-attachment is gone, there is no longer gain or loss. You may ask, "So which is better, gain or loss?" For one who has experienced the ultimate enlightenment, such talk is meaningless.

Yesterday, someone came to tears when he caught a glimpse of the enormity of his self-attachment. When I asked him if he still had attachment, he replied, "Yes, but perhaps a bit less."

I said to him, "Well at least you have lost something. Hopefully by retreat's end you will lose even more. Maybe you will lose so much your fiancée won't recognize you when you return home." It may sound funny, but it is a concern for some practitioners. On a previous retreat, one participant voiced such concern: "If I go on letting go of things, at one point I might lose everything. Who would I be then? What would I be then?" It is no laughing matter. You may find yourself in such a situation some day. Your self-attachment will not allow you to let go without a fight. Whenever you are on the verge of losing something, or have already lost something, there is a natural tendency for fear to arise. And with this fear comes another natural tendency—to try to hold on to something, or even to create a new attachment. This is vexation, a natural response of sentient beings. As a practitioner, be aware of this and know that with continual practice, these fears, expectations, and desires will lessen.

Everything that is active originally was not created refers to any and all phenomena (dharmas), actions, or manifestations. Here are more perplexing lines from the *Song* that seem to contradict common sense. Does it mean that results can spring from nowhere? Can I become a doctor or professor without studying and working for it? That would be ludicrous. It would seem natural to suppose that phenomena arise from something else, from some kind of matter or effort. For instance, this building was created from raw materials and work. It didn't arise from nothing. We cannot say that this building is not created. Obviously, the *Song* is alluding to something else.

Every evening we recite from the liturgy, "To know all the Buddhas of the past, present, and future, perceive that dharmadhatu nature (the dharma realm) is all created by the mind." This is the perspective of ordinary sentient beings. We say that within the dharma realms, everything is created by the mind; phenomena come into being from the individual and collective karma of sentient beings. All things are but the fruition or manifestation of these karmic forces. *Song of Mind*, in saying that all phenomena are originally not created, takes the viewpoint of the enlightened. For the enlightened there are no distinctions to be made. Phenomena still exist, but they are not categorized, rated, judged, or given meaning. It is we who make distinctions between man and woman, fire and water, moral and immoral. For us, these concepts carry different meanings, but the enlightened do not make these self-centered distinctions. Things are just as they are.

It would not even be correct to say that enlightened beings see all dharmas as the one Dharma. For the enlightened, there are no dharmas to speak of. If there were, that would not be the ultimate state. And if there are no dharmas, how can there be creation? It is here where confusion arises. People mistakenly believe that in the enlightened state, there is only emptiness and nothingness. For the enlightened, phenomena still exist, but they are not seen with attachment or discrimination. Hence, this condition is called "no-dharma." One does not reject the existence of phenomena. The phenomena we create—phenomena with constructions, or attachment—still exist.

Buddhadharma does not negate the world and phenomena, nor does it teach people to escape from the world. It teaches people to liberate themselves by affirming the world and at the same time, not attaching to it. The completely enlightened can still exist and fully function in the world. They can and do interact with other sentient beings. And except in rare instances, enlightened beings and Chan patriarchs do not upset the normal order of things.

I read about a preacher from another spiritual tradition in Taiwan. In response to the current controversy regarding the evolution of humans, this man took a monkey to a public area and said, "If it is true that human beings descended from monkeys, then this monkey is a descendant of your ancestors, and you should respect it as such. But if evolution is true, then how come this monkey is still the same, and we have evolved into a higher order of beings?" He also heard that the Buddha speaks of all sentient beings as having buddha-nature. So he collected cats and dogs and insects and preached to the public, "You Buddhists don't have to prostrate to Buddha statues. If all sentient beings are the same, you can prostrate to these animals here." This person has misunderstood Buddhadharma. Enlightened Chan patriarchs and masters still respected the icons and sutras of Buddhism. At the same time, they were aware of and understood that Buddhist statues are not buddhas and that the sutras are not really the Dharma.

Still, stories persist about the strange antics of Chan masters. There is a story about a famous master who was spotted urinating in front of a Buddha statue. Monks saw him and tried to drag him away, saying, "How can you, as a master, act so ignorantly and disrespectfully?" He asked them what he was doing that was wrong and they said, "This is a Buddha statue, a place of the buddhas."

He answered, "Tell me of a place where there is no Buddha and I will urinate there."

This is one of those classic Chan stories that demonstrates the master's efforts to break apart the strong attachments of practitioners and disciples. This was a once-in-a lifetime occurrence. The master chose an opportune moment to make a point. If, on the other hand, he urinated in front of Buddha statues on a regular basis, he would more likely be considered an eccentric rather than a master. Most of the time, enlightened masters will act like ordinary human beings. They will not tamper with the order of things, or human relationships, or commonly accepted principles of action.

As practitioners, you should not be looking to become something different, something that stands out. Imagining what an enlightened person would be like and then acting upon those imaginings is accumulating more baggage, and frivolous baggage at that. Learn from the words spoken here from the *Song*. Adopt its teachings of gain and loss. You can only truly practice when there are no thoughts of gain or loss. If such thoughts are in your mind, all you will gain is vexation. Trying to achieve something to tell people back home is a wrong attitude and a waste of time. Trying to emulate someone else's experience is also a waste of time. Comparing yourself to others leads to feelings of superiority or inferiority, envy or arrogance. Don't even compare your present with your past experiences. All of this is just more vexation, and it is not conducive to good practice. When the situation does not seem good, don't think that you have failed. When the situation seems to be very good, don't think that you have succeeded. Why should you not harbor these so-called positive, motivating thoughts? So as not to cultivate a mind of gain and loss. Of course we should think positive thoughts, but here on retreat do not cling even to this attitude. In each moment, just do your best. Care about what you do but do not cling to whatever happens. The best attitude is to be in the moment and to stay on the method.

6.4 ▪ Let Vexations Go Gradually

> Know that mind is not mind;
> There is no sickness, no medicine.
> When in confusion, you must discard affairs;
> Enlightened, it makes no difference.

How can we arrive at no-mind from our normal, scattered condition, or even from the level of one-mind? There are two Chan methods to attain no-mind: one is silent illumination, the other is gong'an, also known as *huatou*. Both are sudden enlightenment methods. While enlightenment through silent illumination usually starts off shallow and deepens with continued practice, *huatou* usually leads to a more clear-cut enlightenment that may be either shallow or profound.

The *Surangama Sutra* describes a method similar to silent illumination, in which the bodhisattva Avalokitesvara has perfected the hearing sense to perceive intrinsic nature. But since intrinsic nature has no sound, this method is essentially silent illumination.

Master Xuyun ("Empty Cloud"; 1840–1959) described a method of contemplating the pure and intrinsic nature of mind, which has no fixed characteristics. At the moment one truly perceives this, one is a buddha—this mind is buddha, and buddha is this mind. The practice leading to this moment is to turn one's awareness inward, watching and listening. Gradually, vexations and wandering thoughts will diminish and eventually disappear. When all wandering thoughts cease, what remains is the sound of one's intrinsic nature. But this is just an expression, since there is no "sound" of intrinsic nature. Thus, Xuyun's method is also similar to Avalokitesvara's method and to silent illumination. This method being very difficult for beginners to use successfully, they should begin by counting or following the breath. But if one reaches a point where counting or following the breath naturally falls away, then these methods, too, are equivalent to silent illumination.

The method of Avalokitesvara begins by listening to actual sounds, but it is truly realized only when there is no sound to be heard. For now, at your level, do not try to emulate this method. If you are counting breaths, only when the number naturally falls away should you begin to use silent illumination or *huatou*. Dropping the number while still wrestling with wandering thoughts is just deceiving yourself. When you can sit for successive periods using the breathing method with minimal or no overt wandering thoughts, you are approaching the stillness of mind needed to effectively use these other methods. There are no hard and fast rules. With practice, you can even begin right away with *huatou* or silent illumination; it is just easier to begin with the breath and then switch when the mind has somewhat cleared and stilled.

There are many levels to the *huatou* method. For example, with the question, "Who am I?" you can go deeper and deeper until there seems to be nothing left to work on. You may think the *huatou* is finished. At this point, some teachers or schools give a new *huatou*, but it is not necessary. You can still go further. Eventually, something will open up again and you will be able to go even deeper into the *huatou*. Again you may reach a point where there seems to be nothing left to work on, and then a new level will open up. You can even work on one *huatou* for the rest of your life. Even at the moment of death there may still be more levels to work on.

Silent illumination differs from *huatou* in this respect: since you begin with nothing, there is never any sense of reaching a point where there is nothing left to work on, and then having new levels open up. With continued practice you just go deeper and deeper, without seeing the levels.

A *huatou* is actually meaningless and quite uninteresting, like chewing on cotton—tasteless and flat. For a beginner *huatou* is like that—you work with it like a persistent dog chewing cotton, until you begin to savor the method. Investigating a *huatou* with your intellect is a waste of time and effort. Any intellectual answer you come up with is not it. After working very hard you may come up with what seems a profound realization, but that is not it either. I will use another chewing analogy: working on a *huatou* is like chewing on whole grains of rice. At first, all you are doing is chewing the husk, which is without nutrition. You may think you have reached the nourishing part, but you haven't. After breaking through the husk, you think, "I've got it!" But you are just beginning. You now have to chew the rice into finer and finer bits, with the nutrition still locked inside. You continue to chew, even after the rice seems to be gone. Here I must depart from the analogy, because in reality, practice goes even further. You must continue, not only after the rice is gone, but until you, the chewer, are also gone. The practice is complete only when you reach buddhahood.

The Rinzai sect of Zen often has people start with the *huatou* (Jap., *wato*) "*mu*," but for many beginners, this would be little different from counting the breath. It would be no more than recitation because at this point a necessary element is lacking, a genuine doubt in their minds. We are not talking about ordinary doubt, but about a burning, uninterrupted persistence to get to the root of a question that has no answer. It is rare to have this doubt sensation right from the start, and beginners would just repeat the *huatou* over and over like a mantra. Only when the sense of doubt rises does true *huatou* practice begin. The word "*chan*" ("*zen*" in Japanese) has, as part of its meaning, the idea of investigating or questioning. To question or investigate a *huatou* is proper practice, but I advise students to start with breath methods to collect and concentrate their mind before practicing *huatou*.

Some people simply cannot use a *huatou* or silent illumination, often because the flow of their energy (*chi*) makes it difficult for them to stabilize their minds to where the methods can be useful. There are methods for training the mind—such as counting the breath, *huatou*, and silent illumination—and there are methods for training the body and *chi*. However, body and mind are intimately connected, so sometimes the methods for the mind trigger responses in the body. If practitioners learn to properly control or channel their *chi*, practice will flow more smoothly.

When *chi* moves smoothly and harmoniously, one's physical condition will be stable and strong, and the mind will be calmer. This is a good foundation for practice. If you have problems with your *chi*, try to relax and continue to practice. The problem will most likely work itself out. The practice itself will help regulate your *chi*; you are also laying a strong foundation for future practice.

Chi can be felt as many things: movement, a tingling sensation, heat, coolness, pressure, blockage, etc. Sometimes, people experience something they think is *chi*, but is not. For instance, I have advised someone not to use the *huatou* method for the time being, because when he does, he applies too much effort. The result is painful pressure in his head. This is not *chi*, but actual blood flow to the brain. Sometimes bodily heat is created by *chi*, but sometimes it is from another source. For example, even though you are sitting, meditation requires energy, and this can make you hot. Heat can originate in other ways. In samadhi there is a heat that arises and actually evaporates vexations. This kind of heat we can all use.

A common misconception is that to work hard and concentrate, one must tense up and apply a lot of pressure. This can cause your heart to race or your blood pressure to rise. If you are concentrating hard, noticing these changes might worry you. That may in turn cause you to lose your method and also increase your vexation. Therefore, I always say, "Relax your body and mind, but work hard." That means to concentrate without applying tension or pressure. If you feel uncomfortable physiological sensations, do not be alarmed. Just relax. Place your attention on the soles of your feet or at the center of your gravity and relax. Your energy will settle down. When *chi* flows smoothly and harmoniously through your body, you will not be aware of it. You will just feel calm, healthy, alert, vitalized, and energetic, not nervous and fidgety.

The *Song* says, *When in confusion, you must discard affairs; enlightened, it makes no difference.* It is impossible for the confused mind to let go of vexations all at once. The process is to let go gradually in successive stages. First, let go of the past and future. Second, let go of the environment around you. Third, let go of the previous thought and the next thought.

Letting go of the previous thought and the next thought is difficult, because even when there is only one thought, you are still connected to the past, the present, and the future. If you can stop the mind, thus letting go of the past and the future, then the present will also be gone. This is no-mind. After enlightenment there is no need to let go, since there is nothing to be discarded, and nothing to be picked up.

6.5 ▪ No Concern with Gain or Loss

> Originally there is nothing to obtain;
> Now what use is there in discarding?
> When someone claims to see demons,
> We may talk of emptiness, yet the phenomena
> are there.

A practitioner who appears unconcerned with gain or loss may be deeply enlightened or just apathetic. There was a monk at the monastery in Taiwan who, as a youth, was lazy. He had to be prodded and scolded to go to elementary school. The same thing happened with high school. He preferred hanging around in stores and leafing through comic books. How his parents got him to go to college is a mystery, but he reluctantly applied and was accepted into a mediocre school, where he did what he had to and nothing more. He took night classes at a leisurely pace and graduated well after four years. After finishing college he had no desire to do anything. He had already become a monk at the age of twelve. It was my master who accepted him, and then passed him on to me. His attitude was, "I'm already a monk, why bother with anything?"

Of course I scolded him because he did not do his share of the chores. Actually, he did not do much of anything. To an outside observer my approach probably seemed harsh. Other disciples reproached me: "Shifu, you shouldn't scold him. His actions conform to that of an enlightened person. He truly understands that there is nothing that needs to be done in this world. It's we, the unenlightened fools, who run around like chickens without heads, making all kinds of trouble for ourselves. If you don't believe us, look in the *Platform Sutra*, where Huineng says the enlightened person has no likes or dislikes. He can put aside his work and lie down. He can rest."

Well, these disciples were right about one thing. This lazy monk was a first-class sleeper. He had no problem with taking only one meal per day, which was impressive to the other monks, but he was very protective of his sleep. He went to bed earlier and got up later than everyone else. When I questioned him on this, he said, "Shifu, it's not my problem that you concern yourself with work and affairs that you think important. To me they are trivial and not worth my time."

Such trivialities included washing his clothes. He would just use his socks over and over, turning them inside out again and again until they were so unbearable he had to throw them away. When I criticized him in front of others, quite a few disciples defended him: "Shifu, you shouldn't scold him. He has his own reasons, his own perspective."

"What perspective might that be?" I asked.

"It is you and others who feel it is necessary to wash one's feet and socks, but must it be for everyone? Do oxen and cattle worry about washing their feet? They are his feet and socks, not yours. If you think his socks reek, that's your problem, not his."

Eventually, this monk left me. Now he has his own temple! He is actually an easy-going person with a kind nature. Nothing seems to bother him. He is popular with elderly women. Maybe they wash his socks now. So what is the moral of this story? Perhaps I have been a fool my entire life, one of those chickens without a head.

Actually, I tell this story to show you how people can easily be fooled by the actions of others, or even by their own actions. If you look deep enough and twist meanings around enough, you can get the scriptures to justify any of your actions. The point is that if this monk had genuine wisdom, at least some of it would have been recognizable. It is too bad, because he had some good characteristics—his detachment from material wealth and his easy-going nature would have made a good foundation for practice. And, he serves a purpose for people who are drawn to that kind of personality. If you would prefer his style, after this retreat I can give you directions to his temple.

So, when I say that you come to retreat not to gain things but to lose things, I am not extolling the virtues of laziness. By gaining, I mean more attachments and vexations. On the opposite extreme of apathy, trying to gain wisdom by wrestling it under your control only creates expectation and anxiety. Would you think you have failed on this retreat if seven days passed and you never experienced anything to talk about? If that is what you want, you can find such experiences at your local movie theater. If after seven days, you can say that you worked diligently on your method most of the time, then you have succeeded. You may walk away thinking you have gained nothing and lost nothing, but I guarantee you the retreat will have its affect on you. You just may not realize it for a while. I only ask that you make good use of your time and an environment designed for focused, uninterrupted practice. If you just want to spend seven days in a soft, comfortable haze, you are wasting your time. That easygoing monk might be more of what you want in a teacher.

A well-disciplined life is invaluable, and being mindful is more precious than jewels. If being on this retreat can instill in you these values, even for a while, you have not wasted time. All you have to do is practice your method. Perhaps you are thinking, "Isn't becoming disciplined and mindful gaining something?" For people who have not attained no-mind, yes, there is still gain and loss: gain of wisdom, and loss of vexation; gain of merit and virtue, loss of karmic obstructions; gain of clarity, loss of scatteredness and confusion.

If you light a match in a dark room, you can claim that you have added light. However, striking a match outside on a sunny day would not add any light to speak of. You are fundamentally limitless, but only when there is no mind. As long as there is a mind you are bounded. When there is no mind, there is no self and therefore nothing to lose or gain. But when you practice, you begin in the dark room of your ego. You practice to let go of this self-centeredness. When you completely let go of it, that is the state of no-mind. Then there is no longer a dark room to illuminate; you are already in broad daylight.

Buddhadharma offers you guidelines for letting go of this ego. Begin by taking the Four Great Vows, especially the first, which is to deliver all sentient beings. When you think less about your own desires and turn your attention to the needs of others, your self-centeredness will naturally diminish. Acknowledge the existence of other sentient beings and try to act for their sake first. Similarly, recognize and respect the Three Jewels—the Buddha, the Dharma, and the Sangha.

You might be thinking, "I came here to meditate, not save the world. How can I help others if I don't take care of myself first? Especially these innumerable sentient beings the vow speaks of? How can helping others, but not myself, lessen my self-centeredness? In fact, it might make me resentful and miserable, which would make my self-center even harder to bear." It is natural to think these thoughts. When you first begin to practice, it is the Four Great Vows and Three Jewels that are unnatural. In fact, the vows are almost unimaginable in their full meaning. I suggest they are worth your time, even if at first the idea of helping sentient beings is intimidating. When you put on a new suit, at first it is stiff and uncomfortable. You are aware of it and it feels awkward. But eventually it begins to feel more and more comfortable, until it is part of you, like a second skin. After practicing for a long time and having deep experiences, you will understand why the Three Jewels and the Four Great Vows deserve your respect. Your attainment will be proportional to how much respect you have for the Three Jewels, the Four Great Vows, and sentient beings.

Great practitioners can be recognized by their great service. Having no self-attachment, they are also humble. Bodhisattvas are without pride or arrogance. They do not see themselves as helping sentient beings; they are just doing the work of the Three Jewels. In the eyes of a bodhisattva, sentient beings are delivered by their own merit and actions. Am I saving you? Am I delivering you? It is you who are practicing hard. It is you who are changing your attitudes. I am only doing the work of the Three Jewels, but that happens to be my perspective. If you think you owe me something, that is your perspective. Hopefully, you also feel indebted to the Three Jewels. Actually, feeling indebted to me and to the Three Jewels is not a bad thing. Without this attitude, your ego might be swelling with pride: "I meditate, I learn the Dharma, I guide myself through the obstacles of practice, I pull myself along when the going is rough." The goal of practice is to free ourselves from such an attachment to the "I."

The freer we are from attachment to self, the closer we are to attaining a mind of no gain and no loss.

The Sixteenth Karmapa Rinpoche of the Kagyü sect of Tibetan Buddhism once visited Bodhi House on Long Island, New York. A religion professor was showing the rinpoche a collection of sutras in his library. Karmapa did not understand English or Chinese, but when he saw the sutras written in Tibetan, he prostrated three times. Another person in attendance said, "Your Holiness, you are Karmapa. You are ultimately enlightened, the equivalent to the Buddha. These sutras are of no use to you. Why do you prostrate before them?"

In answer, Karmapa prostrated three more times, and when he finished, he said, "Others may say I am a buddha, but I am not a buddha." Without Buddhadharma, we would not know how to practice. Hence, the *Tripitika*, the canon of Buddhist scriptures, is the relic of Buddha's Dharma body. Karmapa of course recognizes this and so has great respect for the sutras.

When someone claims to see demons, we may talk of emptiness, yet the phenomena are there. What or who are these demons the *Song* speaks of? Are they the kind with horns and sharp teeth and pointy tongues? Have you seen such demons? What are the demons in your mind like? The *Surangama Sutra* speaks of many different kinds of demons. There are demons that arise from within your mind and there are demons that come from outside, the so-called heavenly demons. It takes a great practitioner to attract these heavenly demons. You do not have to worry about such demons. You have plenty of your own to keep you occupied, those being the demons created by your own mind.

Demons come in many guises. For instance, you are meditating well, and then suddenly you are filled with thoughts of your spouse. Sometimes the thoughts are so powerful it seems that this person is standing right in front of you. These thoughts and ideas, true or false, are demons that come from your own mind. This does not mean the people in your thoughts are demons. You do not have to scold them when you return home. Your own mind conjures these demons and hinders your practice.

All mental activities that obstruct you are demons. They need not be horrifying or painful. As long as they keep you from practicing, they are demons. You must train your minds by relying on Buddhadharma, which teaches the fundamental principles of the Buddha, as well as how to practice and what methods to practice. Hence, such words or descriptions, even though they are empty, are still of great use.

All the teachings of Buddhadharma are meant to help you reduce your attachment to a self-center. You must first master your own body, then master your own mind. Do not let your body dictate how you will feel. If you feel discomfort from sitting too long in one position, think of it as a pleasant feeling instead, and go on with your practice. If sleepiness seems to overtake you for no reason at all, tell yourself you are not tired and keep practicing. This is being master of your body.

As for controlling your mind, when wandering thoughts come, ignore them. If you find that you are already lost in wandering thoughts, pull your mind back to the method. Actually, everything has to do with the mind—wandering thoughts, pain, itchiness, even the teachings and methods of practice. Fundamentally they are empty. Yet for us they exist; and some, like the teachings and methods, are vitally important.

Don't destroy the emotions of people

7.1 ■ Awareness without Emotion or Attachment

> Don't destroy the emotions of people;
> Only teach the cessation of thoughts.

In this stanza, *emotions* refers to thoughts, dreams, feelings, fantasies, and all other workings of discriminating mind. Mental activity is a human condition following us whether we are engaged in everyday life, asleep, or practicing. After all, daily life is also practice. Someone who has been practicing *shikantaza* for a couple of years said that he was having difficulties with the method. He thought that when doing *shikantaza*, there should be no thoughts in the mind other than the method. I said that regardless of which method one uses, there should not be any thoughts other than of the method itself. For example, when counting breaths the only thoughts in your mind should be those of the breath and the counting. As all who practice know, this level is not easy to attain.

If through practice you reach a state where there are no ordinary thoughts (emotions), then either you have entered deep samadhi, or the thoughts that do arise do not create any desire or aversion. However, the verse refers to the emotions that arise from self-centered discrimination and attachment.

Reaching these levels requires hard work. To make matters worse, if you become attached to samadhi, those feelings are a product of ordinary mind. After first experiencing samadhi, people often crave returning to it, thus creating a new obstacle. Sometimes, for a brief time—perhaps a few seconds—they may think they are not discriminating, that they have reached the level of no-mind. This thought may bring great satisfaction and joy, but this is ordinary mind. What they believed to be no-mind was in fact either indifference, or a mind so unclear that they could not even discern the thoughts that were filling it. The true state of no-mind, and therefore nondiscrimination, is to be clearly aware of what is happening without giving rise to emotions or attachment.

On retreats in country settings I sometimes allow participants to wander outside with instructions to use their eyes and ears, but not their minds. Rarely can someone do that successfully. Sometimes people reach an intermediate stage where what they see and hear is different from what they ordinarily see and hear. Though they cannot explain it, they say that the trees, the sky, and the other people look somehow different.

One reason we meditate is to train ourselves to experience thoughts without corresponding attachments. It is a gradual process that does not proceed linearly from confusion to clarity. You may be clear for one sitting and swamped by wandering thoughts the next. Resenting them only compounds your vexations. When thoughts and vexations come, keep your mind on the method. The mind of vexation comes in many forms, so be aware. It may be "My legs hurt," or "I'm just wasting my time pretending to meditate," or "This feels good; I could sit all day."

On one retreat a young man came to me and said, "Shifu, I have to leave. If I stay any longer I'll end up killing somebody." I asked him whom he was thinking of killing.

"You! You're the person I will kill."

The man was suffering from leg and back pain and he was wallowing in his misfortune. All he could think of was getting back at the person who had made it all possible, me.

So I said, "Fine, this should be easy to fix. I'll give you a knife and you can kill me."

"Well," he said, "I don't feel like killing you right now, and I dare not anyway."

"In that case," I said, "go back to your cushion and continue sitting."

Allowing yourself to be overcome by thoughts and emotions just creates more obstructions. Let them wash through you without attaching to or repelling them. Learn from the lines of the *Song of Mind*—do not try to destroy your emotions, because that is impossible. All you can do is learn to stop the thoughts that are triggered by such ordinary mental activity.

7.2 ▨ Undefiled Mind Can Be Realized

> When thoughts are gone, mind is abolished;
> When mind is gone, action is terminated.

These lines describe the relationship between thoughts and the mind. Thoughts are illusory—they come and go, triggered by emotions and the environment. In turn they set the stage for other thoughts, speech, and actions. It is the illusory mind of ordinary sentient beings that interacts with such thoughts. When thoughts cease, the mind that is abolished is ordinary, defiled mind. Pure, undefiled mind cannot be abolished, since it is not reliant on thoughts and is not illusory. There is no point pondering the difference between defiled and undefiled mind, since to do so we need to use thoughts. We are embedded within the illusory nature of the defiled mind, and we take it to be real. With this defiled mind we perceive the world, express ourselves, have emotions, and act. When we have a defiled mind, we cannot act according to what we imagine to be a pure mind. As long as we rely upon such thoughts, we must accept the existence of the defiled mind and have faith that there is an undefiled mind that can be realized.

On retreat we are all keenly aware of our scattered minds. We may try to distinguish between clear and confused thoughts, but in fact there is no real distinction. In Buddhism, thoughts are by definition confused. A thought that is not confused would not be a thought, it would be wisdom—the functioning of the pure, undefiled mind. By their nature, emotions and thoughts constantly stir us to think and act, thereby creating vexations.

People come to retreat because they know they are deluded. That is a start. People who do not even recognize they are deluded have the more serious problem. Look around you. The world we call "normal" is filled with people controlled by their cravings and aversions, their thoughts clouded, and their emotions in disarray. They run around creating problems for themselves and others. Right outside the Chan Center is a perfect place to observe the confusion and delusion of humanity. One retreatant told me that her friends were worried about her mental health because she was going on a seven-day meditation retreat. They think she needs to see a psychiatrist to help her straighten out. You may laugh. Although we might disagree with her friends' solution, they are not entirely wrong, for we are all deeply deluded.

The difference between thoughts and the mind is that thoughts are always scattered and confused, whereas the mind can be guided, focused, and unified. We progress from scattered mind, to concentrated mind, to one-mind, to no-mind.

The line, *When thoughts are gone, mind is abolished*, seems to imply that we can arrive at no-mind by getting rid of scattered thoughts, but it is not so simple. Thoughts are a function of the conscious, discriminating mind, which can be scattered or concentrated. To have a concentrated mind is already very good, and is a prerequisite to moving on to one-mind and no-mind. If you reach the level of one-mind, however, it is not the end of discrimination. By ordinary standards, it would seem that there is no discrimination at the level of one-mind, but one-mind still has limits and boundaries. For there to be one-mind, the mind must be united with something. Furthermore, to perceive that the mind is united with something indicates that there still exists a certain amount of discrimination. Therefore, one-mind cannot be the ultimate state.

A tenet of Eastern thought is that "one" comes from "two" and "two" comes from "one." Nothingness cannot give rise to something. This concept is clearly illustrated by the familiar yin-yang symbol. Western religions state that a God who existed before anything created everything. In other words, one gives rise to everything else. If one were to ask where this God came from, the answer would be that God was, is, and ever shall be eternally self-existent. Buddhadharma, however, says that something eternal and unchanging cannot give rise to anything else, or be created by something else. If one thing has the capacity to create something else, then it too must have been created. Therefore, one-mind is not absolute and cannot stand by itself. It exists within a framework, just as yin exists within the context of yang, and yang exists within the context of yin. Neither can stand alone, and neither is eternal or unchanging.

In the evening liturgy, we recite the line "To know all the buddhas of the past, present, and future, perceive that *dharmadhatu* nature is all created by the mind." Here, "mind" refers to the mind of discrimination, and *dharmadhatu* nature refers to the countless dharmas, or phenomena, each with characteristics and boundaries. All phenomena are created by the discriminating mind, which generates thoughts and ideas that lead to more thoughts, words, and action. These thoughts, words, and actions become causes of future consequences—good, bad, or neutral—that we must deal with and accept. This is karma—it creates the ever-changing environment in which we act, and in acting, we create more karma. Thus the cycle continues moment after moment, life after life, spinning the wheel of samsara.

When mind is gone, action is terminated means that when the discriminating mind stops, no further acts that create karma are committed, thereby liberating the individual from samsara. Retreat is a time set aside to try to let go of the discriminating mind. Perhaps that sounds a bit frightening. People think that their identity, existence, and worth depend on the existence of discriminating mind. If this mind is abolished, who will you be? Will you be the same? Will you remember your loved ones? Will you be able to return to your regular lives, your families, and your jobs?

Do not worry that you will turn into zombies without thoughts or feelings. Chan retreats are not factories that produce insane people. From the discriminating mind comes confused thoughts and deluded emotions. From the no-mind state comes true wisdom. After Shakyamuni Buddha attained complete enlightenment, he still recognized his family and disciples. He was aware of everything around him. Otherwise, how could we call him wise, and why would anyone have listened to anything he said?

To let go of discriminating mind means to let go of attachment. Through practice, you can begin to let go of attachments and begin to experience liberation. You may not become completely enlightened like the Buddha, but for every moment you can meditate without discrimination, you will be without vexation. The *Song of Mind* speaks of high goals, but we must begin by taking the first step: diligently apply yourself to your method of practice.

7.3 ▦ False and True Emptiness

> No need to confirm emptiness;
> Naturally, there is clear comprehension.

The emptiness that the *Song* and all Buddhist texts speak of does not mean nothingness. Because of this misunderstanding, Buddhism is often considered to be nihilistic and pessimistic. By "emptiness" Buddhism means impermanence, the fact that everything is continually transformed by causes and conditions.

On one retreat I asked someone, "What is your name?"

He replied, "I have no name."

"Who are you?"

"I don't exist, so how could I be somebody?"

"Where are you?"

"If nothing exists, how can I be anywhere?"

The practitioner was not wrong in what he said. He may well have been experiencing those feelings and ideas. Originally, he had no name; it was given to him after he was born. His mother gave birth to his body, but before birth, it did not exist. And it surely is not the same body now that he is an adult. If this is so, then does the body truly exist? And if the body does not exist, how can one speak of a space in which it resides? These are ideas one can philosophically debate and logically deduce, but they are not enlightenment. People who practice without a teacher may misunderstand this meaning and think they are enlightened.

People sometimes go through phases where worldly activities seem boring, insubstantial, and unreal. After a retreat, a woman told me that she did not want to be bothered with her husband and child anymore. I asked, "What is it that you want?" She said, "Nothing, really, but if I thought about it, perhaps I would consider becoming a nun." I said, "But if you become a nun you will still need a master, and later you will probably have disciples." She replied, "No, I don't want that. I just want to become a nun." I said, "If that's your attitude, then you're not qualified to become a nun." After a while, those sentiments faded. She, also, was not experiencing Buddhist emptiness.

The people in these stories illustrate false emptiness. With true emptiness, or ultimate emptiness, everything exists, but one is not attached to anything. The *Heart Sutra* says that the five *skandhas* that constitute the sense of self—form, sensation, perception, volition, and consciousness—are empty. It does not mean that they are apparitions or mirages. What does not exist is what we call the "self." The five *skandhas* exist, but they are without enduring, individual, independent self-natures. Realizing this directly—that is, through the understanding that comes with enlightenment—is to experience true emptiness.

The *Diamond Sutra* says that all dharmas are like dreams, bubbles in water, shadows, and reflections. We can debate this and arrive at some sort of intellectual construct we agree on, but it would only be conjecture. For instance, a wall is real in the sense that it is solid—we can see it, feel it, and hurt ourselves if we run into it. From the Buddhist perspective, however, it is impermanent; it does not exist in and of its own accord, and is therefore not real. Scientists say that matter is essentially a combination of electromagnetic radiation and local densities of subatomic particles, but this too is theory and speculation unless you directly experience it. You will naturally understand the nature of emptiness when your mind is completely unattached from any ideas of self and other.

The *Song* says that there is no need to confirm emptiness—it is not a treasure hidden somewhere outside yourself that needs to be discovered or experienced. It is evident, right here and now, all around and within you. Earlier today, someone farted and the stench filled the room. It may mean that someone's digestion was off, an indication that the person may also not be meditating well, but that was then and this is now. There is no longer a stench. This can happen only if things are empty. Emptiness is the true nature of what we take to be reality.

The *Song* says, *Naturally, there is clear comprehension.* When there are no attachments and obstructions, the mind is clear and instantly understands its own nature. This clarity is often compared to light, but that is a faulty analogy because light does not penetrate everywhere. Where there are obstructions, there is darkness. The clarity of enlightenment has no obstructions. It is clarity of the mind, not of the eye. This clear, bright mind is no-mind, the mind of no attachment.

There is no true enlightenment as long as one takes the five *skandhas* of form, sensation, perception, volition, and consciousness, to be real. Are you attached to your body, your ideas, your ways of thinking, and your feelings? Do you know anyone who is not? It is part of the human experience and it is why we practice, because it helps us to see the true nature of emptiness. One needs only to stay with the method, and attachments will drop, one by one. Gradually, you will perceive all five *skandhas* to be empty, and when you do, you will have attained true freedom.

Thus, we need to distinguish between false and true emptiness. If the examples I gave previously are false kinds of emptiness, what is true emptiness? The answer is that in true emptiness, phenomena exist, but the mind is not attached to anything. In other words, there is no idea of "self." The *Heart Sutra* says that the five *skandhas*, the aggregates that make up our phenomenal existence, do not exist independently. There is nothing there that can really be called a "self."

Question: I think I understand a little bit, but not much. Are you saying that everything is as it is conventionally, but if one is attached to the conventions and does not see it as a kind of mirage, then one is lost?

Sheng Yen: That is basically correct. Again, the *Diamond Sutra* says that all dharmas, all the phenomena that we consider existent, are really illusions, like bubbles in the ocean, or shadows.

Student: It seems to me that the greatest difficulty in Buddhism is seeing that a cup is conventionally real, and at the same time it is not that at all. It is very difficult to keep both aspects in awareness at the same time.

Sheng Yen: When we say that something "doesn't exist," we are basically saying it lacks enduring reality, that it is impermanent. This is what we always have to keep in mind. If we do not do this, then we attribute to phenomena and events, including our bodies and personas, a reality they truly do no have.

Student: This idea that nothing really exists, that all matter is just energy or radiation, has been in Western science and philosophy a long time also. We have that intellectual piece of information, but we do not have the firsthand experience of this truth. How can we get this firsthand experience? I think this is really what we are trying to do.

Sheng Yen: When the mind is totally unattached, this experience will appear by itself, so don't think of emptiness as a thing out there that needs to be experienced. Again, when there is no attachment in the mind, no obstructions, there is naturally clear comprehension. At that point, one understands one's own nature. When this happens, is there anything that is perceived or seen? This kind of clarity can't be compared to sunshine, or any kind of light. Where there is sunlight, things can be seen; where the sunlight does not penetrate, things are in the dark. But there are no obstructions in the kind of clarity referred to here. It is not clarity that you see with the eyes; it is clarity of the mind, a mind of pure awareness.

Let's return to our commentary. We have said that no-mind is a clear mind without attachment. The line, *Naturally, there is clear comprehension*, warns us about experiencing false emptiness. The reason you are not yet liberated is because you take the five *skandhas* to be your true self. You just need to stay with your practice as your attachments fall off one by one. Gradually you will experience clear mind, and see the *skandhas* as truly empty. You have then attained liberation and true freedom.

Are you attached to your body? Are you attached to your ways of thinking? Are you attached to ideas and concepts? Chris's wife Maria will have a baby soon. What kind of baby would they like to have? Chris has probably been thinking about how to educate the baby, how to bring it up as a Buddhist in a Christian country. It's just like the president of the United States, who has a lot of things to think about to keep the country in good order. The same mentality applies to raising a child. There are a lot of problems needing resolution. There is nothing wrong with that, but is this no-mind? What about an attitude like, "I don't care what comes, whether it's a little dog, a little cat, anything." Is this no-mind? That is also incorrect.

However, the attitude of "this is *my* child" is not too good either. Rather, you should see your child as a sentient being—or, looking at it more deeply, as a bodhisattva or buddha coming into this world—and try not to discriminate so much between your children or other people's. Try to have less attachment to what you think belongs to you. Parents' questions about their child's future are all for the good, but it is even better if, in the spirit of Buddhism, they also show concern with children not related to them.

7.4 ■ Every Thought Is a Birth and a Death

> Completely extinguishing birth and death,
> The profound mind enters into principle.

Birth and death, as it is used in the line above, has two meanings, and it is the second meaning that is more important. The first meaning is the birth and death of the physical body. According to Buddhadharma, as long as karma exists for the individual, retribution will manifest as cycles of birth and death. The karma created by following the Five Precepts and performing the Ten Virtuous Deeds can lead to a more fortuitous human birth, or to being reborn in a heavenly realm. The karma created by the Five Hindrances, the Five Hellish Deeds, and the Ten Evil Deeds can lead to a less fortunate human birth, or to rebirth in the less desirable realms of the titans, hungry ghosts, or the various hells.

The second meaning of "birth and death" refers to the birth and death of the mind; that is, when a previous thought perishes, a new one arises. Moment after moment, thoughts arise and perish, ceaselessly. Any thought produced by the three poisons of greed, hatred, or ignorance prolongs the birth and death of the mind. Even thinking, "I want to be a buddha," is created by this mind of birth and death. Aspiring to enlightenment and wanting to follow the bodhisattva path are good, but they are desires nonetheless.

A disciple once asked Master Mazu (709–788), "What is non-birth and non-death, not arising and not passing away?"

Mazu replied, "I don't know. I only know about samsara—the karma of birth and death."

The disciple asked, "Then what is the karma of birth and death?"

Mazu said, "Wanting to be a buddha, wanting enlightenment, wanting to be a bodhisattva, wanting to cultivate the six *paramitas* (virtues perfected by a bodhisattva)."

Our desire to transform ourselves from ordinary sentient beings into buddhas is still a product of the mind that arises and passes away. It is a necessary place to start, but the person who begins with this desire must eventually leave it behind. Huineng said in the *Platform Sutra* that we should begin our practice by taking the Four Great Vows. On retreat we follow his advice and recite the vows several times a day, but when we meditate we should not have these thoughts. Make a vow as you bow to the cushion, but once you sit down and take up the method, let the vow go and allow its power to strengthen and help your practice. Furthermore, do not aspire to too much, such as vowing to sit until you attain enlightenment. Work to your capacity, such as making a vow to sit for the entire period without moving, or promising yourself to sit until your mind clears.

For those working on a *huatou* the same advice applies. Vow to sit until you give rise to the doubt sensation, the burning desire to answer the question posed by the *huatou*. Even if you already have the doubt sensation, vow to sit until it engulfs you and becomes a great ball of doubt.

Actually, when engulfed by the great ball of doubt, you would be so absorbed that you would not want to leave your cushion. This great ball of doubt is a necessary step in *huatou* practice; otherwise the method cannot result in enlightenment.

Many practitioners cannot give rise to this doubt sensation. All they can do is recite the *huatou* over and over. Others give rise to the doubt sensation, but can go no further. Sometimes, a practitioner in the midst of this doubt will have a wandering thought, and mistakes it for the answer to the *huatou*. This may in turn be mistaken for enlightenment. Breaking through a *huatou* does not mean that you have found an answer; what it means is that in dedicating yourself to finding an answer, you have left the self behind.

On one retreat, someone was using the *huatou,* "Who am I?" Suddenly he stood up, walked over to me, and said, "I know the answer. I'm that little rock on the table under the painting of Bodhidharma."

I asked, "How come you are not Bodhidharma, just a little rock?"

He replied, "Well, I don't know. I was practicing hard and felt compelled to turn my head. When I did, the first thing I saw was the rock, and the thought came to me: I am the little rock."

Do not laugh, it could happen to you. This kind of response is common. Throughout Chan history people have been practicing *huatous.* Books recount exchanges between masters and disciples. One can read about the answers that disciples gave, whether as words or actions. People have been reading these books for centuries, hoping to gain insight into the methods. Many give those same or other clever responses, but it is a foolish waste of time and just skirts the practice. The truth is, there are no correct answers. When you are truly working hard on the method, and you reach a point where there are no thoughts at all, then you can see your buddha-nature. That is the only correct answer.

And now I have a question. Is there a mind that sees buddha-nature, or is it no-mind that sees buddha-nature? If you can correctly answer this, you will have seen into your self-nature.

7.5 ▓ No Mind, No Environment

> Opening your eyes and seeing forms,
> Mind arises in accord with the environment.

We encourage beginners to meditate with their eyes open, so that they do not succumb as easily to drowsiness or fantasies. On the other hand, some choose to close their eyes because the environment distracts them. Actually, it doesn't matter, because wandering thoughts and fantasies will arise, drowsiness will come, and the environment will at times distract you. The problem is not with the eyes but with the mind.

Many people tell me that their fantasies are never as vivid and beautiful as when they come on retreat. Some say that they can create a beautiful scene on the wall in front of them, travel into the scene, and

interact with it. I tell them that I am happy the Chan Center can pro-
vide them with such fine entertainment, but that they might make bet-
ter use of their time by concentrating on their practice. For those who
like to indulge in such illusions, meditation seems to have benefits, but
here it is a waste of time.

If you open your eyes when meditating, do not focus on anything,
which means not using your eyes to discriminate, or to attach to wander-
ing thoughts. In daily life, if you are engrossed in a book, a movie, or
your work, you become unaware of everything else. I ask that you apply
the same single-mindedness to practice, so that everything else fades
away. Of course, counting breaths is probably not as interesting as read-
ing a novel, or daydreaming about exotic islands, but that is why medita-
tion is called practice.

The same is true for all your other senses. When something captures
your attention, through whichever sense, your mind has been ensnared by
the phenomenon. It is no longer your own, and it is impossible for you
to be its master. When you hear a beautiful sound, your ears want to
draw closer to it, and the same is true for other sense objects.

In all cases, the mind is being led and swayed by the environment.
Originally, the mind doesn't exist, but when the eyes look at something,
the mind arises, and when the ears hear something, the mind also arises.
However, if you do not use the sense of sight, the mind of looking does
not arise, and so on for the other senses. That is why I ask you to isolate
yourself from the environment, both outside and within the Chan Cen-
ter. By concentrating wholeheartedly on your method, you will not pay
attention to what is around you, and your mind will not be moved by
your senses. As you are well aware, this is not as easy. Even if you success-
fully disengage your mind from the five physical senses, there is still the
sixth sense of discriminating consciousness. Your mind continues to be
swayed by memories and thoughts, by the past and future.

Where is the mind of the cook who is still chopping vegetables even
though she is now meditating? Where is the mind of the mother who,
while meditating, daydreams of playing with her child? Whatever you
like to do in your daily life, chances are your mind will be doing it while
you meditate, calling up the memories and entrapping you. Some of you

are watching movies; some of you are playing music; some of you are writing stories; some of you are playing sports. Some of you are solving problems at work; some of you are planning vacations; some of you are replaying what you said and should have said in last week's argument. Have I missed anything? It is part of the human condition. That is why I also encourage you to isolate yourself from the past and future. This is necessary to disengage the mind from the sixth sense of discriminating consciousness.

The mind originally does not exist. It arises through contact with the environment. Not only must there be an environment, but one must perceive and interact with it. If contact, perception, and interaction do not take place, the mind will not arise. Furthermore, if there is no interaction, the environment will not exist either. Apart from the mind there is no environment. It is someone else's environment, someone else's phenomena. At that time even your body is not yours. It too is someone else's perception, phenomenon, and environment.

During meditation we draw our minds back from the environment—from space, time, past, and future. If and when you effectively isolate yourself, the mind will not arise. At that time, I ask you, "Where is your mind, what is your mind, who are you?"

You may insist that an objective environment must exist whether someone is cognizant of it or not. But if there is an objective environment, then there must also be a subject. One cannot exist without the other. Does that mean that if your mind stops while you are doing fast-walking meditation, and you forget to make the turn at the end of the room, you will walk right through the wall? No. The point is that if your mind stops, you probably wouldn't be walking anymore. It is not uncommon for people who achieve this state to collapse during walking meditation. I say probably, because some people continue to walk after their minds stop. Their bodies continue to move out of habit. The same thing occurs when people reach this level of absorption during prostration. Some people will freeze in position, others will continue to rhythmically move.

Mind-stopping also occurs in samadhi, but there are many levels of samadhi. There is also a past and future with samadhi, though a person in this state may not be aware of time. Time is still present because a person can move into and out of different levels of samadhi, and because there is still a self on which the meditator reflects. Therefore, one cannot say that the self, the past, and the future disappear in samadhi. Subject and object still exist in the one-mind state, except the subject has expanded to include all other things. In samadhi one is not aware of the environment, while in the no-mind state, one is clearly aware of the environment—phenomena remain but attachment to self is gone. Through meditation we want to reach a point where the mind does not arise. When there is no mind, at that time there is no self. If that condition lasts indefinitely, we say that such a person is liberated.

The two existing sects in Chan Buddhism, the Linji (Jap., Rinzai), and the Caodong (Jap., Soto), may use different methods, but their goal is the same: to reach a point where the mind does not arise. The Caodong sect uses silent illumination, in which the meditator "just sits" until all thoughts fade and the mind no longer arises. The Linji sect uses a *huatou* to concentrate the mind, create the doubt sensation, and then burst apart all thoughts so that the mind does not arise. The meditator's persistence in trying to penetrate the *huatou* is like a mosquito trying to draw blood from an iron bull. If the mosquito persists, it will eventually disappear, just as the diligent *huatou* practitioner's sense of self will also disappear.

Intellectually this all sounds fathomable, reasonable, even doable, but it isn't easy. From the ego's point of view, it is the same as asking it to die. And if the mind is the self, it is like asking the self to die. Are you willing to die? If you say yes, then practice should be no problem. Enlightenment is just around the corner. But talk is cheap, and speculation that does not lead to action is idle chatter. I ask again if you are willing to die to become enlightened, because that is what it takes.

Of course I am talking about the death of your ego, your attachment to self. I am not referring to the death of your body and life. When the self dies, you are still here, the world is still here. Your life is still your life. Nothing changes except that your attachment to self no longer exists. But when you stand at the threshold of enlightenment, these words offer no assurance or consolation. To enter the gate of Chan you must let go of your body and mind. As far as your ego is concerned, that means death.

Practice is the way to gradually loosen our attachments to the world and to our selves. On retreats we practice with intensity, using our methods in a controlled environment. In daily life you can still practice, you can meditate, and you can be mindful. It does not mean cutting yourself off from the environment and withdrawing your senses. You are still aware of everything; you appreciate beauty, avert danger, and so on. The practice is in letting phenomena (objects, ideas, feelings) come and go without clinging to them, without dwelling on, or indulging in them. The same is true when you meditate—don't deal with your thoughts and emotions by suppressing or denying them. Simply observe them coming and going, like the wind. You have no choice. As long as you are a sentient being with vexations, thoughts and emotions are going to arise.

Within mind there is no environment

8.1 ■ Experiencing Mind and Environment

> Within mind there is no environment;
> Within the environment there is no mind.
> Use mind to extinguish the environment
> And both will be disturbed.

The lines, *Within mind there is no environment, within the environment there is no mind*, describe a deep level of practice. We are normally aware of, and interact with, our external environment. The noises, sights, and smells influence our thoughts. Hence, there also exists within our minds an internal environment. There are three levels at which practitioners may experience mind and its environment. At the first level, mind and environment are in contrast. At the second level, mind and environment are experienced as separate. At the third level, in the environment there is no mind, and in the mind there is no environment.

At the first level, where we begin our practice, the mind either is drawn to or repelled by the environment. If you are hungry, the scraping of a spatula in a wok may suddenly seem louder and more insistent, and the odors of cooking may be so strong that you might imagine the chef to be right next to you. In this case the sounds and smells of cooking *are* your environment, and it is your mind that notices them. If your legs hurt, pain is your environment and again it is your mind that notices it. Whatever attracts your attention becomes your environment, whether it is discomfort, sleepiness, your own movements, and so on. If you are so sleepy you don't even notice it, then at that time there is no environment for you. But when you are alert to everything, your awareness becomes your environment. That is the meaning of mind and environment being in contrast to one another.

Since practice begins at this first level, you need to pick one object upon which to focus and settle your mind. This becomes your meditation method, and if you persist, it will become your environment. If wandering thoughts intrude on your method, then that becomes your environment. Thus, beginning cultivation means learning to control your mind's environment rather than being swept up in an endless stream of wandering thoughts.

At the second level there is no environment—only the mind exists. There is an environment only if the six sense organs come in contact with the six sense objects, giving rise to the six sense consciousnesses. The six sense organs are eye, ear, nose, tongue, body, and discriminating mind. The six sense objects are forms and colors, sounds, scents, flavors, objects, and symbols. The six sense consciousnesses are seeing, hearing, smelling, tasting, touching, and thinking. The environment manifests when our sense organs come in contact with the physical world, which our discriminating mind then perceives, giving rise to the six sense consciousnesses. But the activities of the mind—thinking, feeling, and remembering—are also an environment. One can be isolated from the physical world and still interact with a mental one created by memories, ideas, and emotions. Anyone who meditates knows that the mental environment can be infinitely richer and more distracting than the physical one. Therefore, as long as one engages in discriminating thoughts, one has not separated mind from environment.

In shallow samadhi, light and sound are still perceived. If they still exist in one's mind, then mind and environment are not separate. In still shallower samadhi, one may perceive the heavenly realms or the Buddha's Pure Land in all their beauty and splendor. This is a joyful experience, but it is not separation of mind and environment. One must attain deeper levels of samadhi before the environment ceases to exist for you.

At the deeper levels of samadhi, one feels liberated, but this indicates that there is someone who can be liberated, and therefore the mind still exists. Even so, these are profound levels of absorption equivalent to the deepest levels of one-mind. As with samadhi, Chan speaks of different levels of unified mind. Shallowest is unity of mind and body, deeper is unity of the external and the internal, and the deepest is unity of space and time. Even at the second stage, where one feels unity with the universe, there is still a perception of universality. Although one no longer discriminates between mind and environment, environment still exists, and so the two are still not separate. Only when space and time are unified does one truly experience separation of mind and environment.

Within mind there is no environment; within the environment there is no mind describes the no-mind of Chan, in which there is no attachment to self and its vexations of greed, hatred, and ignorance. Master Huangbo (d. 850) said something along these lines: "I exist and the environment exists, but the environment has nothing to do with me." This is not an easy level to attain. Would you remain unaffected if I scolded you harshly? Would you acknowledge my words without being disturbed? Being easily swayed by our physical and mental environments, we must begin at the first level.

The *Song* then says, *Use the mind to extinguish the environment and both will be disturbed.* Because beginners are easily distracted by the physical environment, they try to oppose it: "Those damn car horns! That incense smells good. The guy next to me keeps moving." How do you deal with these outside phenomena? If you see them as disturbances, they have already affected you. Shutting them out of your mind will only make matters worse. Instead of relaxing and focusing your attention and energy on your method, you will get tense and use your energy fighting your senses and thoughts. The slightest sounds and movements will then distract you.

To make the environment disappear pay no attention to it, whether it's a pleasant or unpleasant situation. Some people try to resist the environment or cast out wandering thoughts; others lose faith in themselves and simply give up. Both kinds of responses come from letting the environment affect you. Reactions of anger, frustration, joy, boredom, or bliss—whether to your surroundings, or your practice—also mean that you have let the environment affect you. The solution is to simply tend to your method and allow all other situations, thoughts, and feelings come and go as they please.

8.2 ▪ What Moves? Flag, Wind, or Mind?

> With mind still and environment thus,
> Not discarding, not grasping,

When the mind is unmoving, the environment is also unmoving; but though the environment is "thus," both it and the mind still exist. In other words, where there is mind, there will also be environment. There is a deep samadhi in which only mind exists, but Chan does not advocate practicing this for its own sake. The purpose of Chan is to realize wisdom, but for wisdom to function, both mind and environment must exist, since the undefiled mind arises from the environment in the first place.

When the *Song* says that the environment is "thus," it does not mean that the environment becomes static. Everything still exists and flows, but because the mind has no attachments, the environment, reflecting the mind, is also unmoving.

A story in the *Platform Sutra* of Sixth Patriarch Huineng speaks to this point. At the gates of a temple, the master encountered two monks who were discussing a flag fluttering in the wind. One monk said, "I say that the flag is moving." The other said, "No, actually it is the wind that is moving." Huineng interrupted them and said, "It is neither flag nor wind, but your minds that are moving."

Common sense tells us that the flag is moving, and also that the wind causes the flag to move. The patriarch obviously knew this, but he saw an opportunity to help the monks. For those accomplished in cultivation, the issue of flag or wind moving has nothing to do with them.

At the end of the Southern Song dynasty (1127–1279), an invading army was moving south. The news reached the villages and people fled. As everyone scrambled to escape, a monk named Chu-yuan said, "If it is time for me to die, I will die, but if I am not destined to die, I will not." So he stayed put.

When the army arrived at the monastery, the invading general told Chu-yuan, "If you are still here, that means you are not afraid to die. If that is true, then it does not matter if I kill you."

The monk said, "Take good care of the long swords of your dynasty. In the shadow of lightning you kill the spring wind."

To Chu-yuan, the general's decision to kill him or not was no more than spring wind in the shadow of lightning. His mind was truly unmoving, and not affected by the environment.

To reach this level of cultivation is extremely difficult, but possible, and it will occur gradually and naturally through practice. It would be impossible to attain this level of realization after just a few retreats, but we can at least begin to learn not to be so affected by what happens around us. For example, while meditating, you should not be disturbed if someone walks by you, laughs, cries, screams, or is hit by the incense board.

Last week during evening meditation, the silence was broken by loud knocking and insistent ringing of the doorbell. Finally, Nancy answered the door, and a large angry man using vulgar language wanted to come in. Although Nancy seemed a bit timid, she did not overreact. I was meditating too, and when I looked up, I saw everyone else still sitting. Some of the students were also big and strong, but no one made a move to get up. To me that was a good sign of solid practice. In the end it was I who could not keep still, so I got up and asked the biggest man in the group to help out. At that point, he calmly got up and went to the door to help Nancy appease the man and persuade him to leave peacefully.

One must start practicing somewhere, and not being affected by the environment is a good start. This, however, is not the unmoving mind. If it were, the unmoving mind would be a dead mind. A truly enlightened person still takes care of ordinary business, but his or her mind is not affected by the external environment, and does not generate passions or vexations.

What is the meaning of *Not discarding, not grasping*? Most of the time, people want to discard what they dislike and cling to what they like. In both cases the mind is being moved by the environment. If one's mind is unmoving, then ideas of rejecting or clinging do not arise. Today, someone in interview asked me why I tell people to let go of good feelings and experiences. Wanting to hold on to a good experience causes the good feeling to go away. The best way to maintain good feelings is by not attaching to them. Feelings of comfort and discomfort are just aspects of your environment. Whatever moves you, whether drowsiness or energy, pain or joy, anxiety or serenity, is just part of your environment.

Therefore, I urge you to neither attach to good experiences, nor reject bad ones. Just accept and let go. To the enlightened there is no discarding or grasping. They may lose their loved ones, their houses may crumble, their fortunes may disappear; they may have an abundance of love, and they may amass a huge fortune, but in any and all cases they remain unaffected. We cannot expect to be at this level after a brief time of cultivation. Here, people often complain about pains in their legs and backs. It is true that pain is rarely comfortable, but an enlightened person would say that it has nothing to do with him or her. Pain is "thus" and nothing more, but if we have karmic obstructions, then we suffer because of it.

There is a modern-day story of a layman who was beaten to the point of death by hoodlums, but harbored neither hatred nor resentment. Instead he said, "This old fellow has too much bad karma. Maybe some of it got beaten away." This man is a good example of one who has learned to not hold on to anything. When you are meditating, do not be moved by anything that happens. Do not hold on to anything, and do not reject anything.

Mind Following Environment

> Environment is extinguished together with mind.
> Mind disappears together with environment.

There are three stages of practice, during which the mind's relationship to its environment changes. In the first stage, mind follows environment. In the second stage, environment moves in accordance with mind. In the third stage, described in the lines above, environment is extinguished together with mind, and mind disappears together with environment. The two lines mean the same thing.

The first stage of mind—following environment—is our condition most of the time. When our minds are turned by phenomena, the sight of a beautiful landscape, or the sound of a brook—it is mind that follows environment. In identifying with these phenomena, we are turned or influenced by them. If the phenomenon is sufficiently compelling, we can become so immersed that we lose our identities during that time. In practice you can use this to your advantage. Lose yourself in your method—whether it is *huatou*, counting breaths, or walking meditation— the way you might lose yourself in a fascinating novel. Allow your mind to identify completely with the environment created by your method.

Many practitioners complain that pains in their legs and back disturb their concentration and throw them off their practice. If this is an obstacle you feel you cannot overcome, then take advantage of your environment. Make observing your pain your method. If you do this until you identify completely with it, the pain will abate. This is good beginning practice.

Some people still have trouble with wandering thoughts after several days of retreat. This can lead to frustration, which exacerbates the problem. If you cannot still your mind, try putting aside your usual method and catalog your wandering thoughts instead, to see which ones occupy your mind the most. Perhaps they are the ones that relate to your job, your partner, or your child. One student cannot get her four-year-old daughter out of her mind. I told her to make her daughter her method by repeating over and over again, "I have a four-year-old daughter, I have a four-year-old daughter. . . ." If this helps, it is as good as reciting Amitabha Buddha's name. Also, as she identifies more and more with the phrase, her preoccupation with her daughter during meditation will lessen and, perhaps, eventually disappear. I have a feeling many of you are considering using this method.

If you allow phenomena to pull you away from your focus, you will lose clarity and control of your conscious mind. Instead of drowning in stimulation, let the environment help you focus by choosing one phenomenon, and making that your method.

Environment Follows Mind

The second stage, where environment follows mind, shows that the mind's power can be strong. People with great mental power are able to influence their environment. When long-time practitioners come to me with problems, I often suggest that they use their mind power to help change their situation. Like meditation, this requires diligence before you will see any results.

Great practitioners are able to use their mind power to change other people's mental attitudes, but they usually refrain from doing so, as it can cause more harm than good. It tends to frighten people because they think they are being brainwashed. In Taiwan, a woman asked me if I could influence her husband to stop having an affair with his mistress. I told her that I would talk to the man if she wished, but that I didn't have any power to change his mind or course of action. Nonetheless, the man never came to see me because he was afraid I would exert some kind of influence over him, and he did not want to end the affair. However, if in fact I did have such powers, I would be able to influence his behavior whether he came to see me or not. If I really had such a reputation, I would never get any rest.

More important is how you can use your mind to influence the environment. For instance, one practitioner may be disturbed by another every time he sees her. He can tell himself, "she is not real; she is just a shadow." Objectively the environment has not changed, but he has changed his attitude to it. Besides, who is to determine what an "objective" environment is?

We can use our imaginations to change our perceptions of the environment, such as seeing adversaries as bodhisattvas helping us in our practice. In this manner we are thankful for, and perceive all phenomena and all relations, as helping our practice. It is due to our attachments, which are products of our impure minds, that we like and dislike things. In the same way, we can use imagination to change our reactions to such phenomena. If your legs hurt after sitting a while, you can tell yourself, "Any minute now, the pain will subside, and my legs will feel nice and cool." This may seem like self-deception, but it is really autosuggestion, and can be useful. In changing your own mind and attitude, you also change your environment.

All the same, letting go is the best way to deal with disturbances, especially ones that come up suddenly. If you are startled by a buzzer, your annoyance should only last just for a moment or two. If you hold on to that annoyance after the buzzer has stopped ringing, then you have let the environment affect you.

When the Mind Is Extinguished

The third stage of mind in relation to the environment is described in the lines, *Environment is extinguished together with mind, mind disappears together with environment*. When mind is extinguished, the environment also is extinguished. Conversely, when the environment disappears, mind also disappears. Buddhadharma speaks of two kinds of mind: that of vexation and discrimination, and that of purity and wisdom. But there is a dilemma here, for if Buddhadharma speaks of a mind of purity, how can it disappear when the environment disappears? The Buddha also spoke of two types of wisdom: fundamental wisdom and acquired wisdom. Fundamental wisdom is unmoving, neither arising nor perishing under any circumstances. Acquired wisdom, on the other hand, arises in accordance with the needs of sentient beings. Acquired wisdom arises when environment arises, and disappears when environment disappears. It arises to help sentient beings. If there were no need or no sentient beings, then it would not arise.

Wisdom is not always what people imagine, and the responses of enlightened beings don't always correspond with the desires and expectations of sentient beings. As analogies I will offer two anecdotes from my life. It isn't necessarily true that all Chan masters act or even look like great practitioners. People are often fooled or disappointed by their appearances and behavior. One of my two lineage masters, Lingyuan, was such a man. Even in his eighties he did not have the demeanor some may expect of a great master, yet he was. Lingyuan looked like an ordinary monk, perhaps a bit oafish. When he spoke he did not dispel that opinion, because he was neither eloquent nor articulate. He was not charismatic. The few times in his last years that I visited him at his temple, some of his disciples pulled me aside and said, "Master Sheng Yen, why don't you teach us?"

I would reply, "Why would you want me to teach you when you have this great master right here?"

They would say, "Well, he looks sort of stupid and he doesn't know anything."

I told them that they were missing a great opportunity because of their expectations and preconceptions. Then I told them a story: About thirty years earlier, Lingyuan and nine other venerable monks were invited to preside over a precepts-taking ceremony for newly ordained monks and nuns. The other nine monks were dressed in ceremonial robes and had attendants, but Lingyuan came unattended and had with him only a small, ragged cloth bag to hold his few travel items. Instead of using the main entrance he entered through the side door. When it was time for lunch and everyone was seated, no one could find Lingyuan. Finally, someone from the kitchen came out and said that no one was around except for an old monk who had asked for some left-overs, which they gave him. Sure enough, when others went to the kitchen they discovered that it was Master Lingyuan. The kitchen monk was extremely embarrassed and said to the master, "I'm sorry. We didn't know who you were. How can you ask for leftover food?"

Master Lingyuan said, "What does it matter? This food is good enough for me." The truth is, Master Lingyuan was a great master. On the other hand, I have known other masters who were charismatic and glib speakers, but who had problems with their conceptions of the Dharma and with their behavior.

Here's the second anecdote. Once a man from Canada called and told me he wanted to stay with me so he could witness and learn firsthand what he had heard from others. I said, "No, better not do that. Seeing me is worse than hearing about me." But the man insisted and eventually came to our Center.

I asked, "What do you think I can possibly teach you?"

The man obviously did not understand me, because after spending a few hours at the Center, he started to complain.

"Why don't you teach me something?"

I said, "If you want to stay here a while, that is fine, but there is nothing I can teach you. When I eat, you'll eat with me. If I perform a service, you will perform it with me. When I go to sleep, so will you. This is what I do."

Originally he had intended to stay for a week, but by the second day he left. He probably thought I did not have anything to give him. For him, I suppose that was true.

In no way am I suggesting that either Master Lingyuan or I are enlightened. These misconceptions happen on every level. Therefore, although acquired wisdom may be manifesting all around you every day, you may not recognize it as such.

8.3 ■ Tranquil Quiescence

> When neither arises,
> There is tranquillity and limitless brightness.

When neither mind nor environment arises, there is tranquillity and limitless illumination; vexation disappears and wisdom manifests. For ordinary beings, environment and mind are poles that coexist. When wisdom manifests for the enlightened person, there is no mind, and there is no vexation; there is also no environment. Wisdom is not a product of the mind of discrimination, which dualistically posits an "I" and an "other." When the mind distinguishes between "this" and "that," there is always vexation. On the other hand, wisdom simply illuminates without dualisms, and therefore does not give rise to vexation.

People make judgments: this is good, that is bad; this is beautiful, that is ugly. Upon what criteria do we base these and countless other dualisms? How reliable is our personal, subjective judgment? Is it in accordance with the agreed-upon standards of a nation, and if not, are we wrong and they right? Does a majority or consensus make something true or correct?

The United States judicial system is based on the premise that people are innocent until proven guilty. Of course the system, like any other, is flawed; innocent people are sometimes punished and so-called culprits get away with their deeds. The point is that the United States has a system that most of its people agree upon. But other countries have judicial systems that are based on the opposite premise, of guilty until proven innocent. Who is right? Here we contemplate an issue by setting up polar concepts. Perhaps one could find an issue that most people agree on, but it might be at odds with the ideas from another era. In the end, as long as there are positions and standpoints, there can be no such thing as an absolutely correct judgment. Correctness itself exists only in relation to incorrectness.

As long as there is a dualism of mind and environment, perceptions and judgments will never be completely reliable or true, and vexation will be part of the process. This is true with individuals, among families, within nations, philosophies, and religions. Throughout history, governments and religions have based their ethics and laws on their own criteria, and thus affected the thoughts, words, and behavior of people. None of them are absolutely right, reliable, or unchanging. Buddhism is one of these institutions, but it recognizes its own limitations. The teachings of Buddhadharma and the practice of Chan seek to liberate us from a dualistic mentality. It is only when the mind is free from dualism and distinction that vexations will disappear and one will enter into tranquil quiescence.

Tranquil quiescence is that condition in which vexations do not arise, where there is no distinction between objective and subjective. In this Chan state of mind there is only natural phenomena and natural existence. To get to where we make no distinctions, we start by making distinctions. This is all we know. Before practice even begins, people must distinguish between good and bad within as broad a conventional view as possible. Once people begin to follow the principles of the Buddha, then they can make distinctions between that which is Buddhadharma and that which is not. Then they must decide whether to practice or not to practice. Further, they must decide what branch of Buddhism to follow and what method to use.

People who have a cursory understanding of Buddhism may decide that it is not necessary to practice. They call upon the quotes of a few ancient masters to support their belief, but they are really only deceiving themselves and others. It is unrealistic to assume that one can make progress on the Buddha path without some type of practice or method. Once a lay Buddhist came to our temple in Taiwan obviously drunk and smoking a cigarette. I approached him and said, "You know that you can't smoke in here, and it's obvious you've had a few drinks too many, so why don't you go home and come back tomorrow?" He objected vehemently, saying that Chan preaches that every dharma is Buddhadharma, that there is no distinction between the Buddha and sentient beings, between drunk and sober, between this and that. He scolded me for not following the principles of Buddhadharma and said I had too much attachment. I said to him, "Okay then, what if I ask my disciples to remove all your clothes and take all your money, and then you can come or go as you please?"

The man was incensed. "Who do you think you are? My money belongs to me. And anyway, if you take my clothes and money, how will I get home?"

I said, "You just scolded me for having attachments, so I assumed you didn't have any. After all, Hanshan, the legendary practitioner from Cold Mountain, never bothered to wear any clothes."

After this, the man began to understand what I was trying to say, so I repeated our rules about not smoking in the temple. He still did not like it, but he left. This man had little understanding of the Dharma, and no idea of proper practice. Obviously, he had heard somewhere that Chan practitioners are supposed to have no attachments, and he was distorting these ideas to justify his own beliefs and behavior. That is why in the beginning, it is important to make a distinction between what is and what is not proper Dharma and the correct path of practice.

Set Reasonable Standards for Self and Others

Do not overestimate yourself. Recognize that you are an ordinary sentient being. If you expect yourself to act like a saint, you will surely be disappointed. You may even decide that the Dharma and practice are not for you. It is equally important not to expect too much of others. In the case of my anecdote, the drunken man expected me to conform to his ideas of behavior and nonattachment. If I followed this man's advice I suppose it would be all right for me to smoke and drink, eat meat, and get married; but then I would no longer be a monk.

As long as we are ordinary sentient beings, we should use the standards of sentient beings. Even if you are a sage, in dealing with sentient beings you should use their standards. Therefore, it is best to set reasonable goals and standards for yourself. If your criteria are too high, ultimately you will become disillusioned and possibly abandon your practice. If your criteria are too high for others, then you will not find or trust anyone to be a good practitioner or teacher, and you will be unable to learn from anyone.

Someone almost left the retreat today. He told me that when he saw everyone sitting so well, he became disillusioned and felt he was wasting his time and mine. I said, "You look at others and assume they are practicing well. Maybe others are looking at you and thinking the same thing." This man's standards and expectations are unrealistic. What does he think good practice is?

Babies on the Buddha Path

Remember that we are ordinary sentient beings, beginners on the buddha path. We are like babies learning to walk; we stand, wobble, and fall; we stand, take a few steps, and fall again. We cry out of frustration. We look around to see if anyone is paying attention. We get up and try again. Some days are better than others, but eventually we improve, until it becomes easier and more natural. When you come to a retreat, don't imagine yourself to be a world-class athlete training for the Olympics. Rather, imagine that you have just started to crawl.

When we begin to practice, it is necessary to make certain distinctions. We must recognize that we are just sentient beings, not enlightened masters and definitely not buddhas. We must also recognize that we are at the beginning stages of practice. I am telling you to make distinctions, so obviously none of you have reached the stage described by the verses above. If one were truly at the level of neither environment nor mind arising, then there would be no need for you to meditate, or for me to lecture. In fact, if you were at this level, there would be no me to speak. Accept that we are baby practitioners learning to crawl, and that with each step we are getting closer to that goal.

8.4 ▦ According with Dharma Is the Bodhi Path

> The reflection of bodhi appears
> In the eternally clear water of mind.

"Bodhi" has multiple meanings in Buddhism. Sometimes it is used in the same way as the "Dao" or the "path." But it can also mean "the end of the path." This should not seem contradictory, for I have often said that the goal of the path is the process. The unenlightened are told that there is a goal to attain, but for the enlightened, who have awakened to the Dao, there is no Dao. *The reflection of bodhi appears* refers to one's practice while on the bodhi path. Apart from practice, there is no bodhi, just as without a body, there can be no reflection of a body. By "practice" I mean more than meditating, prostrating, and all the activities that are considered formal practice. Anything done mindfully and in accordance with Buddhadharma is following the bodhi path. On the other hand, there is no bodhi for enlightened beings (who have already awakened to it) because there is no longer any distinctive effort, nor any notion that they are practicing. Bodhi is known only to those determined to follow the path of bodhi. As one follows this path, one's practice will deepen, and the path will widen and widen until the path disappears. This is awakening to bodhi. At this point, there is longer reflection, there being nothing left to reflect.

One student told me that sometimes he feels that he is progressing, and at other times, he is regressing. He does not feel that his practice is smooth and consistent. But he comes on Chan retreats again and again, and every time the retreat seems good for him. This is a person who has gotten a good taste of practice and who is treading the bodhi path. If it were not so, he would not have the disposition to continue. Another student has never been able to leave behind her steady stream of wandering thoughts, yet rarely misses a retreat. People like these have accepted the Dharma and have strong determination to walk the bodhi path. They know very well that they come with problems and illusions, both in their daily lives and in their practice. They also know that they are benefiting and will continue to benefit. Such an attitude is a good foundation for practice. I am more concerned about the people who come to retreats and think they have no problems whatsoever. These people are thoroughly confused.

The line, *In the eternally clear water of mind*, addresses this issue. If the mind is relatively clear, then problems that arise will be easier to spot, just as in clear water one can see the bottom, the fish, the stones, bubbles, and water plants. But if the water is murky like the Yellow River, one can see nothing but murkiness.

Those in clearer waters, who are more aware of their problems, understand the necessity of practice. Those who think they have no problems are prone to being filled with pride. I see even within the sangha some who think they are the equals of buddhas, bodhisattvas, and saints. A monk who in his youth studied and practiced under my guidance visited me not too long ago. He is a good person, but immediately I knew he had gotten stuck somewhere when he said, "Shifu, should I still prostrate to you?" It is customary for monks and nuns to prostrate to their past and present Dharma teachers.

I replied, "No, that isn't necessary." Then I continued, "In the last few years you must have made great gains in your practice."

The monk said, "Yes, I did have numerous experiences, and they were not bad."

I asked what method he had been using, and he replied, "Methods I learned from others turned out to be useless. In the end, it was a method I invented myself that was the most useful."

I said, "I guess you are ready to become a patriarch since you have discovered a new method of practice."

He said, "What's wrong with that? After all, Shakyamuni Buddha didn't need a buddha to help him attain enlightenment."

I changed the subject and said, "Is there any special reason why you have come to see me this time?"

The monk replied, "No, nothing special. I just came to see if you had attained a higher level of practice."

I said, "Since you have come to see me, I should say a few words. First, to answer your question, I haven't made any high attainments. You however, are in a bad situation. You have fallen prey to your own delusions and have come under the influence of what we call demons. I do not envy your position."

Of course, he didn't like what I said and left. Soon after, I heard that he had left the sangha, and had returned to lay life. This is an instance of one's mind being murky. In this particular case, the murkiness stemmed from the monk's tremendous attachment to attainment. Because of his strong desire to attain something, he fell into this delusive state. It would be wise to heed this story and be vigilant so that you do not find yourselves in similar circumstances.

In the eternally clear water of mind can be understood on two levels. The first is being clearly aware of one's vexations, the second is being thoroughly enlightened. At this level the water truly is eternally clear. In this water there is no bottom, no banks, no surface, no murkiness; there is nothing but water. There is no sense that it is even water. Here, water refers to the power of wisdom, and like the water, this wisdom is pervasive. It is the wisdom of the Buddha, the place where there is no subjective or objective anymore.

Even the first level is not easy to attain. Although many of us know that we have problems and vexations, it is an altogether different thing to say that we are keenly aware of our vexations as they arise. Such clarity only comes when one has seen one's self-nature. Of course, this ability is not like an on/off switch. As we practice, we gradually become more aware of our vexations as they arise, and notice vexations we never thought we had before. As practice deepens so too does this awareness. When finally one sees into one's self-nature, this skill will become very great as long as one continues to practice.

Wisdom Has Nothing to Show

> The nature of merit is like a simpleton:
> It does not establish closeness and distance.

If you have attained the Dao and your mind is in accordance with buddha-nature, it does not necessarily mean that others will perceive you to be wise and charismatic. To others, in fact, you may seem like a fool.

Buddha-nature accords with that which is pure and unmoving. But if it is pure and unmoving, then there is nothing to show. A person whose mind was in accordance with buddha-nature would not stand out in a crowd. Those that society deems intelligent and charismatic are only superficially wise. In regard to worldly wisdom, there is a saying that one who is truly wise may appear to others as foolish. If this is so in the worldly realm, how much more so for someone who has attained the wisdom of buddha-nature? Such wisdom has nothing to show.

In *It does not establish closeness and distance,* "closeness" refers to that which you like and are intimate with. "Distance" refers to that which has not much to do with you. Those enlightened to bodhi see all dharmas as equal. They do not make distinctions between high and low, superior and inferior, near and far. A while back, someone said to me, "I have listened to many of your lectures, and you constantly speak of the Dharma as making no distinctions, and seeing everything as equal. It's a nice idea, but I cannot do it. Even if I could, it would cause nothing but trouble. I cannot see my children and the children of others in the same way. I pay all my attention and give all my love and care to my children. I'm not capable of doing the same for all children. They have their own parents to take care of them. Furthermore, my wife is my wife, so she is someone special. I give her special attention and care. I cannot love other women as I do my wife."

This man's dilemma is similar to the hypothetical situations people often use to discuss ethics and morality: If you had one slice of bread and there were several hungry people, whom would you give it to? Or, if several people were drowning, whom would you save first? Theoretically, one can say whatever seems most fair, but in a real-life situation, theory often goes out the window and we deal with things on an emotional level.

The correct way to think about this idea of closeness and distance is as follows: if you are in need of help, so long as I can provide that help, I will help you, no matter what the relationship is between us. Perhaps there will be situations where I cannot help you, but that is because I do not have the ability to help you, not because we have no relationship. If I have only a limited amount of food, I must first feed my family, because as head of the household that is my responsibility.

If I have the ability to help more people, then I will do so, regardless of whether I know them or not, whether they are close or distant. Whether you have been good, bad, or neutral to me bears no influence on my actions. When Shakyamuni Buddha's father died, Shakyamuni went to the funeral and helped carry his father's body. He did not say that all fathers were his father and spend all of his time carrying dead men's bodies at funerals.

All sentient beings are equal to your parents, but your parents are still your parents. On the other hand, as Buddhists we do not vow to deliver only our parents. We vow to deliver all sentient beings. All dharmas are equal, but each dharma has its own place. According to Buddhadharma, one dharma is not better or higher or closer than another dharma, but each dharma has its own position, its own direction, and its own causes and conditions. The Buddha helped many sentient beings, but he never left India, so no Chinese ever received the benefit of Buddhadharma during Shakyamuni's lifetime. Even in the India of the Buddha's time, many people never heard about Buddhadharma. It does not mean that Shakyamuni Buddha had a preferential attitude toward certain sentient beings. Buddha helped whomever he could help.

Use these lines of verse to help you in your practice. Cultivate a mind like clear water so that you are always aware of your wandering thoughts, and vigilant about vexations arising. But do not simple-mindedly feel aversion toward some thoughts and attraction to others. Meet every condition like the deeply wise person who seems like a fool to others. Do not distinguish between good and bad, close and distant. To the wise fool, all dharmas are equal. You may be wondering why I talk so much, given that I am a teacher of a so-called wordless wisdom like Chan. It is ironic. Because none of us are wise fools, I must use words of distinction to help us move from the level of distinction to the level of no-distinction. I am using poison to relieve the suffering of poison.

Favor and disgrace do not change it

9.1 ▓ Choosing One's Abode

> Favor and disgrace do not change it;
> It doesn't choose its abode.

Most people would agree that pleasant situations tend to make us happy, and stressful ones tend to make us unhappy. However, on a Chan retreat the first step is to develop a sense of calm and equanimity, regardless of circumstances. When things that we like or dislike vex us, we say our minds "follow the environment." On the other hand, if our minds remain clear and unmoving in all situations, we say the "environment follows the mind."

Today is the first day of retreat. How do you like it so far? Are you adjusting to the schedule and rules? Do you like where you are sitting? Are your cushions comfortable? How are your sleeping quarters? Do people bother you while you are meditating, or while trying to sleep at night? These are all questions that occur to a distracted mind.

Our retreats are designed to minimize disturbances, but the truth is that over the next seven days, one thing or another will disturb most of you. These two lines of the Song offer excellent advice: whether meditating, walking, stretching, working, eating, washing, or sleeping, do not allow your minds to follow the environment. You may not be able to control your surroundings, but you should be able to control your minds.

When the mind is not under control, it will be disturbed or distracted no matter how carefully we design the retreat. We once tried to solve the problem of two loud-snoring men by letting them sleep together in one of the more isolated rooms. It did not matter. In the morning each one complained about the noise made by the other.

Disturbances can happen even in the seeming quiet of the Chan Hall. One woman always came on retreats with a large shawl. Once, a woman sitting next to her complained during interview that the shawl always brushed her when the other woman wrapped herself with it before sitting. She told me that she could not concentrate with this woman and her shawl next to her. I told her this was actually an opportunity to cultivate patience. After the retreat she thanked the woman with the shawl for giving her an opportunity to learn patience.

At a retreat in Taiwan, two ladies sharing a room respected the no-talking rule, but one constantly gestured to the other, such as asking her to massage her back. During work time while everyone else did their tasks, these women would be in their room doing massage. On the third day one of the women complained, "Shifu, I can't take it anymore. What did I get myself into? If this continues, I'll never be able to sit well on this retreat."

I said, "You don't have to do these things for her."

She answered, "Yes, I know, but when she begs me to do this and that, I don't know how to get out of it."

What would you do? Would it be easy for you to ignore a fellow practitioner who is in pain and asking you for help? I imagine that for some this would be stressful. What I told the woman I also say to you: this is a Chan retreat, not daily life. Use your time wisely. You have come to devote seven days to intense practice. That is your primary responsibility, your only concern.

These women should have been working like everyone else, but situations like these arise all the time. It takes some wisdom to deal with them, but I will make it easier for you by telling you what to do. In any and all situations pay no attention to what goes on around you. You are here to do whatever is proper on Chan retreats. And if you are like the woman who had the nagging pain, or any other problem, you should seek help from me or from one of the attendants. That is our responsibility. We will help you to resolve the problem.

I remember one young woman who participated in another retreat in Taiwan. She was extremely helpful and enthusiastic. Every time people came to the door, she would jump up and greet them. Though it was not her job, whenever she thought I needed something she would try to help me. Finally I took her aside and said, "With your attitude, you will have a difficult time getting through this retreat. You are not the receptionist or my attendant. I see that you are a very nice, helpful person, but this is not proper behavior for a Chan retreat. In helping others, you are not taking care of your own practice. After the retreat you can go back to helping others again."

While you practice, your mind is to be turned inward, not outward. Do not concern yourself with other people and their affairs, habits, or problems. Your mind is to be focused on your method of practice or whatever else you are assigned to do. If you are continuously attentive to your method, nothing should disturb you.

During retreat there should be nothing to like and nothing to dislike. There are no good seats or bad seats. Everything is as it is and no matter what the situation, everything is exactly right. The structure and schedule of the retreat are meant to make practice as smooth as possible. For example, there are rules about how we are to use our eyes. For the most part you are to give your physical eyes a vacation and rely on the eyes of your mind. Use your physical eyes only as much as you have to for safety. Other than work periods, the only time you should use your eyes is when I am speaking to you, such as during lectures or interviews.

On a Chan retreat it is best to just follow the rules and accept whatever situation arises. Leave your discriminating, judgmental mind behind. In fact, it would be better to also leave your self behind. Thinking about yourself and your own opinions, you will undoubtedly have conflicts, and this will cause vexation. For example, today the rice was not cooked properly, and so it did not taste that good; but when eating on retreat, you should just accept the rice as it is and eat it. Dwelling on the idea that the rice is not good is vexation.

On the other hand, do not entertain thoughts like, "Oh, this is delicious! I can't wait to eat more." Being hungry is physiological, and some people have better appetites, but to entertain greedy thoughts about food is also vexation. From the beginning of the retreat to the end of retreat, let go of your usual conceptions about your self, your wants, and your needs. For the next seven days there is only the Chan Hall and your method of practice. If you preoccupy yourself with all the goings-on around you, instead of curbing vexations you will create more.

The first step on any retreat is to isolate yourself from the external environment. The next step is to let go of your likes and dislikes, your opinions and discriminating mind. Just be concerned with your method of practice. Even if a fire breaks out in the building, it is not your concern. Ignore it and continue with your method, even at risk of burning to ashes. This is true Chan spirit.

9.2 ■ "So, How's My Husband Doing?"

> All connections suddenly cease;
> Everything is forgotten.

All connections refers to the ways we relate to phenomena. First, we relate to things and thoughts that are external to us and have nothing to do with us. It should be easy to disregard such phenomena, but people still dwell on them, not minding their own business, and certainly not practicing. There is a Chinese saying about "a dog chasing a mouse." It is a cat's job to chase mice, not a dog's. Dwelling on things that have nothing to do with you—especially during retreat—is a waste of time.

Next, things happen that we do not deliberately pursue—the thousand-and-one things that randomly happen, such as bumping into a stranger on the street, or dropping a fork at the dinner table. We normally don't dwell upon these happenings. We should obviously not dwell on them during retreat either, but since they are closer to home, so to speak, they are more difficult to ignore than the first kind.

The third way we relate to things is by actively pursuing them. These include thoughts about loved ones, our job, or what's happening during retreat. How many of you can honestly say you have so far not thought once about someone outside this retreat? Such thoughts arise naturally and seemingly endlessly, and they are the hardest to let go.

A couple came to the last retreat, and I told them I was going to seat them so they would not be able to see each other. I told them they should not even think about each other. Both replied, "No problem. We have been married for so many years, the last thing we want to do is think about each other during the retreat." It sounded promising, but during personal interview on the second day, the woman asked, "So, how's my husband doing?"

I answered, "That's funny, just a few minutes ago, your husband was asking the same thing about you."

Can thinking about your spouse, partner, or child on retreat actually do anything for them? All it does is add trouble to your practice. These examples do not exclude those who do not have close relationships. The mind can dwell on all sorts of irrelevant thoughts. I am sure that many of you have already sat through entire periods pondering nonsense.

All Connections Suddenly Cease

All connections suddenly cease can be understood on two levels. The basic level speaks to beginning practitioners, which we all are, and it encourages us to drop any thoughts generated by the three ways of relating to phenomena. It is a basic goal of practice. If you can do this, whether for one second, ten seconds, five minutes, or one hour, it is a sign that your mind is on your method and not wandering.

The second, more profound meaning refers to the experience of enlightenment in which all connections to phenomena are severed. *Everything is forgotten* encourages practitioners to empty their minds while they meditate. If anything remains, it means that they have not dropped all connections. This is not an easy level to reach, but it can happen, whether your method is counting breaths, *huatou*, silent illumination, or reciting the Buddha's name. When counting breaths you may get to a point where you are no longer aware of your breath and no longer counting. You have no thoughts, yet you are clear and aware of everything. This is one of the stages of which the *Song* speaks.

The purpose of a *huatou* is to generate the doubt sensation. However, sometimes a practitioner will just repeat the *huatou* until it spontaneously disappears, without the doubt ever arising. The method has dropped off, yet the mind is clear, bright, and very much aware. This is not the goal of *huatou* practice, which is to experience enlightenment, but it is still a good sign of progress.

Shikantaza is the Japanese Zen term for silent illumination, and translates as "just sitting." The method involves just being aware of one's posture, allowing all other thoughts to come and go without clinging or rejecting. At first you will follow your thoughts and your mind will wander. Eventually you will be clearly watching your thoughts without engaging them. Gradually the thoughts will disappear like silt settling in a pond, and the water becomes so clear you are not aware that it is water. Again, this is a level of mental clarity where all connections cease and everything is forgotten.

Reciting the Buddha's name is one of the five methods for stilling the mind. One can get to a stage where the recitation disappears and all that remains is clear awareness. Of course, this can only happen when one has no more wandering thoughts. Needless to say, forgetting to recite the Buddha's name because you are too busy thinking about your vacation plans does not count.

If one cannot reach a level where no thoughts remain and all external connections cease, then repeating a *huatou* can be quite dry, even meaningless. For this reason many during the late Ming dynasty started to recite the Buddha's name as a method of practice. They felt that if they could neither reach a level where there are no thoughts, nor give rise to the doubt sensation, then they might as well recite something that has meaning and earns merit. Perhaps cultivation of such good karma would allow them to be reborn in the Pure Land, where conditions are perfect for Buddhist practice. On the other hand, if they did reach a point where all connections and thoughts cease, they would be at the perfect point of awareness and calmness to begin practicing *huatou*. At that point they could switch from reciting Buddha's name to asking, "Who recites the Buddha's name?" thus turning the method into a *huatou*.

It is important to understand that reaching a state where there are no thoughts is not enlightenment. It is the first level of ceasing all connections, and is only a preliminary stage. Actually, it marks the threshold where true Chan meditation and contemplation begin. Up to this point all methods are just ways to collect, calm, and concentrate the mind.

At the second level, that of enlightenment, where all connections to phenomena have been severed, there are no thoughts, and vexations have also disappeared. Very few individuals have ever bypassed the first level and jumped right to the second. We cannot all be of the caliber of the young Huineng who became enlightened while hearing someone quote from the *Diamond Sutra*. Most of us need to work on the first level, that of gathering, focusing, and stilling our minds. For most of us, that is our practice.

9.3 ▓ Dark Day, Sunny Day, No Problem

> Eternal day is like night,
> Eternal night, like day.

As with the previous lines, these lines also speak of two levels—that of the beginning practitioner, which includes all of us, and that of the enlightened being. Let's talk about the first level because it is more relevant to our situation. John tells me that so far, every day of retreat has been good. Some of you may feel envious on hearing this, but actually John should not feel too happy about his situation. In fact it would be better if he treated every day as if it were the darkest night. On the other hand, those who feel the days have been dark and difficult should think of each day as being filled with light and joy. If you are wondering how pain can be joyful, know that pain is part of life and that practice is an opportunity to observe pain, accept it, and let it go.

A good lay Buddhist friend in Taiwan with whom I often speak sometimes hears me talk about my difficulties and problems. His response is always, "No problem! Everything is fine." He believes that problems and troubles arise so that we can face them as well as ourselves. It is an important part of daily practice. This man has a great attitude. No matter what happens, it is not a problem. If you have been fired from your job, no problem. If someone you love just died, no problem.

The last time I saw my friend, I had the opportunity to offer him a bit of his own wisdom. What he thought was a promising business venture turned out to be a scam and his so-called partner made off with his half of the investment. "No problem," I said.

"No problem?" he answered, bewildered and scratching his head. "But I've just lost a great deal of money."

I replied, "That's fine. When you have money, you are constantly worrying about how to protect or invest it. It just makes trouble. Now you have nothing to think about, so you have no problems."

There is another story that was popular in Taiwanese tabloids for a while. It seems that the beautiful young wife of a rich and famous man ran away with an American. Of course the press was merciless with her. Everyone sympathized with the man, assuming he was sad, angry, and humiliated. But he seemed unfazed by it all. His friends asked incredulously, "How can you be so detached?"

He answered, "The very fact that others desire my wife must mean that she is a very good woman. It just shows that I have good taste."

Three months later his wife returned to him. Again, the press made a big deal about the turn of events, but the man was still unfazed. He hosted a huge party to welcome his wife back. Again, his friends were quite surprised and asked him how he could be so forgiving. He told them, "That she returned to me tells me that I am a good husband, and that she cares for me. After having the opportunity to compare our relationship with another, she chose me, and that makes me glad."

Is this man wise or foolish? Who is to judge? How can one know his true feelings? I believe this man truly does not overly attach to things, that he had the ability to put things down. This attitude is healthy, and it is relevant to our practice. If you think your leg pains could not get any worse, see it as a golden opportunity to experience such a condition. To experience something you think is beyond your capability is worthwhile. Enduring severe pain tempers your will, determination, and self-discipline. There are different ways to deal with pain, but from the aspect of practice, learn to accept it and then let it go.

Such an attitude works for situations that are painful and difficult, as well as pleasurable and smooth. Therefore, if everything seems to be going exceedingly well with your practice, there is no reason to feel happy or proud. From experience I can tell you: at the moment you acknowledge your good fortune and happiness, the situation will change. Again, if you accept and endure your pain, eventually the pain will disappear and you will be left with a cool, pleasant sensation. The best thing would be to ignore the new development and concentrate on your method. But if you turn your attention to your legs, thinking, "Wow, what an amazing experience! A minute ago my legs were excruciatingly painful, but now the feeling is almost pleasurable. Can this really have happened or is it my imagination? Do I have special powers? Is this a result of good practice?" In focusing on your good experience, you will lose the method and the pain will probably return.

The lesson here is not to let your mind stir either with suffering or with joy. Most of you have probably watched in awe as a circus acrobat performed on a high wire. Where do you think this person's focus is? Is she wondering if the audience likes her act? Is she anticipating applause or hisses? Or is her mind on her performance? Like the acrobat, we must thoroughly train ourselves to be completely unconcerned about what goes on around us or what responses we might encounter, and remain diligently focused on our practice.

To summarize the first level of understanding, these verses tell us not to be dismayed by difficult situations, nor misled by good ones. Like life, practice is not linear; you will encounter good days and bad days, good sittings and bad sittings, good experiences and bad experiences. The best approach is to keep your mind on the task at hand and let the experiences come and go. As practitioners, we should maintain equanimity and not allow our minds to be pulled by the environment.

Eternal day is like night, eternal night, like day also speaks of the enlightened state. Enlightened people do not act differently than the rest of us. People who put on airs because they think they are enlightened are in fact not enlightened. The truly enlightened person does not attach to the experience of enlightenment. It is something that has already passed. For the enlightened, there is really no such thing as enlightenment.

Thus, enlightened ones act more or less like ordinary people. They would likely not stand out in a crowd because they are not concerned with what others think of them. They do not require attention and adulation. Very often a monk who appears slow and dull is a great practitioner, while equally often, one who appears sharp and knowledgeable needs to practice more. Do not waste time wondering what your experiences mean, whether you are making progress, or how you appear to others or to me. Stay with your method and the rest will take care of itself.

9.4 ▣ Outward Foolishness, Inward Clarity

> Outwardly like a complete fool,
> Inwardly mind is empty and real.

I have talked about how some monks who appear to be foolish or dull may actually be deeply enlightened. There are many stories in Buddhist history of enlightened monks who were overlooked by others because of their behavior or appearance. Often these monks would break or disregard many of the minor monastic rules, making them appear to be disrespectful, ignorant, or even absent-minded.

One such story involves Master Hanshan and his encounter with a monk while visiting a monastery. This monk had a disease that grotesquely bloated him and turned his skin a sickening yellow. Because the other monks in the monastery shunned him, the sick monk spent most of his time alone. Still he was grateful for being in the monastery. When he asked for a work, he was given the task of cleaning the bathrooms.

Impressed by how spotlessly clean the bathrooms were, Master Hanshan inquired about it. He was directed to speak to the sick monk, who told Hanshan that he cleaned the bathrooms every night because he had nowhere to sleep. After finishing his chores he would meditate in the Chan Hall until the morning service. Upon hearing this Hanshan felt great respect for the monk.

As it turned out, Hanshan had some long-standing problems with his own meditation. He thought that there might be more to this monk than suspected, so Hanshan asked him for guidance. Hanshan's intuitions were correct, because the sick monk gave him some very good advice on his meditation problems.

We can gain a few insights from this story. This monk felt no need to advertise his experience and attainment, and he also was not deterred by the way the other monks treated him. In other words, he did not indulge in arrogance or self-pity. How would you be affected in similar circumstances? Would profound spiritual experiences fill you with pride? How would you react to constant ridicule and harassment? Worse, how would you feel about being ignored and shunned? Would you have the same resolve and equanimity as this monk?

Usually, the more deeply enlightened a person is, the less he or she will stand out in a crowd. Once, someone made a long pilgrimage to Master Xuyun's residence in order to meet that great contemporary Chan master. The man spotted an old monk spreading manure in a field and asked if he was going the right way, and how long it would be before he arrived at Xuyun's monastery. The monk in the field annoyed the traveler because he asked questions about his reasons for wanting to visit Xuyun. The traveler did not want to be bothered by this ordinary monk, and as you may have guessed, the manure-spreading monk was Xuyun himself.

My own master, Lingyuan, also did not have the appearance of a great, awe-inspiring monk. I myself receive more respect now than when I was younger. Some may say it is because of my personality and reputation as a Chan teacher, but I suspect it has more to do with looking old and my hair turning white.

These two lines of verse refer to the appearance of one who is already enlightened, but I encourage all of you not to wait for enlightenment to cultivate such an attitude. You will have far fewer vexations with the attitude of the diseased monk in the Hanshan story. Pretension brings many problems. If you believe in the rightness of what you do, don't worry about approval or disapproval from others, or whether you look like a fool. Nor should you waste time and energy impressing or getting ahead of others.

Would you consider it below you to get a job as a cleaner of bathrooms? Would you let someone else get the better of you in certain situations? If you cannot do even this, then you have not learned much from practice. If you are clearly aware of what is happening around you, it does not matter if you appear to be foolish or gullible to others. In your mind you know you are not. Having such a manner can also be transforming for others if they eventually realize you are not a fool—your ordinariness will allow them to be more honest and less pretentious.

One of my students told me that he is clear and sharp when he hears my lectures, but when he is working he feels dull, one step behind everyone else. Then he said to me, "You often appear like that yourself, Shifu. If I didn't already know you, I would think that you were stupid."

I did not expect such a comment, and so I responded, "A person with great wisdom is like a fool." But then I added, "Since I'm not a person of great wisdom, you are probably right. Perhaps I am just a fool." After much practice, I have grown less sensitive to things other people say and do; otherwise, I probably would have found this man's comment insulting. Actually, I am sometimes slow. I could claim that is because I am mindful of my decisions and movements, but the truth is, sometimes I do not know what to do. Once, two of my disciples were arguing right in front of me. If I had adhered to the rules of the temple, I would have asked them to leave. Instead I just closed my eyes and sat there, did nothing, and then left.

The same person who said I sometimes acted stupidly witnessed this episode, caught me in the hallway, and asked, "You are their shifu. What are you going to do about it?"

I said, "I don't know." Ultimately I talked to each disciple, but not until they had finished arguing and had calmed down. I would have accomplished nothing trying to reason with them in the middle of a fight. By waiting until they were calm and rational, I could talk to them without shaming or antagonizing them. Also, because they were clearer, the problem was easily resolved. I don't know if I was being foolish or wise, but it seemed to be the expedient thing to do.

In an earlier lecture, I asked what you would do if the Chan Center caught fire. I went on to say that a practitioner with true Chan spirit would continue to stay on the method, even at risk of burning to ashes. I hope you realize that I was exaggerating to make a point. I was encouraging all of you to disregard any and all outside disturbances. On the other hand, you must have enough sense to know what to do in any given situation. If it becomes obvious that the fire is out of control, what are you going to do? If you continue to meditate, thinking, "The Chan Center's Dharma protectors will take care of the situation," then I would say you really are a fool. Do what is expedient. Later if I yell at you for having allowed yourself to be moved by the environment, just accept it. In your mind you know you were clear and that you did the wise thing. It does not matter what I think about you.

In daily life we should train ourselves to be less sensitive to the perceptions of others. Like enlightened beings, do not be afraid to appear outwardly foolish. When you find yourself embarrassed or oversensitive, reflect on why you are not cultivating outward foolishness and inward clarity. This is not an easy task for most people, even for Buddhists. Moreover, we are not enlightened beings, so we cannot expect to act this way all the time. But it is definitely an attitude worth cultivating, and I encourage you to integrate it in your daily life.

9.5 ▪ Think of Practice as Stringing Pearls

> Those not moved by the environment
> Are strong and great.

Those not moved by the three kinds of phenomena—phenomena not related to you, phenomena that happen in a random way, and phenomena that you actively pursue—are considered strong and great. An example of a phenomenon that you actively and willfully engage might be the pain in your legs. Pain in the legs is a physical phenomenon, but the thoughts derived from that pain are a product of your discriminating, self-centered mind. Pain is pain, but the mind that experiences the pain will either remain calm or become vexed.

It is difficult not to be influenced by the environment. Today, was anyone able to meditate, do yoga, eat, work, prostrate, do walking meditation, listen to lectures, recite the liturgy, or even rest without being disturbed by the environment? At the end of the day, do not be ashamed to realize that you were sometimes off your method, or often unmindful. Practice is precisely catching yourself engaging in thoughts of past and future, and bringing yourself back to your method or the task at hand.

Every situation is an opportunity for practice. For instance, does the ticking of a clock disturb you, or do you use it to help your practice? For most, the even, rhythmical sound of a clock is not a hindrance. That is good, but what about a team of construction workers digging up the sidewalk outside? This actually happened when our Center was located across the street. It was a particularly hot and muggy summer retreat. That Center was not as luxurious as this one. What little ventilation we had came through open windows and a noisy fan. For seven days we were surrounded by the sounds of jackhammers, hydraulic machinery, power tools, and workers talking, yelling, laughing, cursing, and telling stories. Two of them ate lunch every day right outside one of the windows, and we all heard their conversations. It was challenging, to say the least. How many of you would have remained undisturbed through all of that? Would you have been able to use that commotion to help your practice?

One of you has said that you would deal with external disturbances by grabbing hold of your mind and *chi*. That will not work. If you grab hold of your mind, it will hurt. If you grab hold of your *chi*, it will become obstructed. What you must do is grab hold of your method. If you are really concentrated, you will not be bothered by any outside phenomena, no matter how chaotic it might seem.

How many of you are aware of me when I walk behind your meditating bodies? If your awareness of me moves you to think, then your mind is scattered. If you are aware of me but continue undisturbed, then your mind is fairly, but not deeply, concentrated. If you were completely unaware of my presence, that would be a deeper level of concentration. One of you has indicated that you are sometimes unaware of my movements. Strange. If you are unaware of my movements, then how can you be sure I was even there?

For the first few days, retreatants are usually easily disturbed by movements, sounds, and pain. As the retreat continues, your concentration will strengthen and deepen. You will acknowledge but not be bothered by things that disturbed you at first. I would describe this as moderate concentration. In deep concentration or samadhi, you would not even note or acknowledge external phenomena.

Think of your practice as stringing pearls, each pearl indicating your attention to the method. As your concentration deepens, the spaces between each pearl—those times when your mind is idle or not on the method—will lessen and eventually disappear. When there are no longer any gaps in your concentration, you will not be moved by the environment.

Of course, the unmoving mind I have described here is different from the unmoving mind of an enlightened being. As with previous verses, these lines can be interpreted on two levels: that of ordinary practitioners and that of enlightened beings. I am sure you all have been completely unaware of phenomena around you when you were totally focused on something. You do not need to practice meditation to experience this. People engrossed in reading, writing, studying, working, or attending a performance can become so absorbed that they are not aware of their environment. These are examples of a non-enlightened mind that is unmoved by the environment.

I recall seeing a movie in which a child was watching an outdoor performance. The boy was outside the periphery of the audience, and he had been tending a small fire to keep warm. He was so engrossed in the show that he forgot the fire, which started to spread and scorch the back of his clothes. Still, he was so involved in the performance that he did not realize what was happening. Part of his awareness knew something was amiss because he would occasionally wave his hand to shoo away the disturbance, but he never once lost his focus on the performance. His clothes ignited, and still he was unaware. His concentration was finally broken by a bucket of cold water thrown on him by someone. If you can work and attain the same degree of concentration as that boy, you have reached a fairly deep level of concentration.

The second interpretation describes enlightened beings who have let go of all attachments. When there is no self-center or mind of attachment, there is no mind to be moved. On the other hand, enlightened beings are very clear about all that happens around them. As the *Diamond*

Sutra states, "The mind should be kept independent of any thoughts that arise within it." The mind that the *Diamond Sutra* speaks of is not the self-centered mind of vexation, but the mind of wisdom. The objective environment exists, but there is no longer a self that attaches to it.

The unmoving mind of enlightenment is different from the ordinary mind that is unmoved by disturbances. Actually, the mind that is wholly concentrated on the method is bound to the environment. In this case, however, the environment is the method. Although the mind is focused and working hard on the method, it is still a discriminating, self-centered mind. Hence, the mind that moves is the mind of discrimination; and where there is discrimination, there is vexation. If discrimination and vexation still exist, so too does the self. Enlightened beings have no attachment to self, and though the environment objectively still exists for them, they do not perceive it as such, since they have no attachments to it.

Those not moved by the environment are strong and great does not refer to people who are famous leaders, athletes, or karate experts. It refers to those without self-centers who are truly strong because they cannot be deterred by anything or anyone. One who is self-centered can still be harmed or influenced by others; but a selfless, enlightened being cannot. Such strength and greatness can sometimes be observed even among unenlightened people. For example, people who act for the benefit of others are often more courageous than those who act only in their own interest. Their words and actions are often more noble. Acting always and only with one's own benefit in mind—even if it is striving for enlightenment—is not a sign of strength and greatness. That is why the first bodhisattva vow states, "I vow to deliver innumerable sentient beings."

While we travel the bodhisattva path we are still ordinary sentient beings, replete with vexation, attachment, and egos. There is still the idea of wanting to help sentient beings, and there is still a sense of satisfaction when we see the good work we have done. This is good, but it is not enlightenment. As the *Diamond Sutra* also states, for those who have attained great enlightenment, helping still continues, but there is no longer an "I" who helps nor sentient beings who need to be helped.

There are neither people nor seeing

10.1 ▓ No Others to See, No Self to See Them

> There are neither people nor seeing.
> Without seeing there is constant appearance.

Neither people nor seeing recalls a passage in the *Diamond Sutra* that says there are neither self nor sentient beings. *Neither people* refers to there being no objective reality. *Nor seeing* refers to there being no self-view, or subjective reality. *Without seeing there is constant appearance* means that even though there is neither self (subject) nor other (object), everything is clearly perceived as it is. When there is no "you" working on the method, and no method being used, we say that you have become one with the method. And though there is neither "you" nor method, you are still working hard from moment to moment.

People on retreat cultivate their minds for an intense and extended period of time. For most, meditating an hour or two a day at home does not provide enough momentum to deeply penetrate a method. As we meditate sitting after sitting, we make the environment as well as our minds become smaller and smaller, until there are no others to see and no self that sees them.

I understand that some retreatants are making phone calls and waiting for family members to arrive so that they can receive and deliver messages. People who have been on retreat before know that this is not permitted, and for good reason. If we cannot even remove ourselves from contact with the outside world for seven days, how can we make our minds and the environment smaller?

The first condition for a successful retreat is to isolate yourself from all thoughts about anything outside the Chan Hall. The second condition is to let go of all thoughts about what happens in the Chan Hall. If someone's yawning makes you yawn too, you are not free from your environment. Train yourself to remember that you have no relationship to people sitting around you. They are they and you are you. I see that someone is dozing while I am lecturing. What do you think? Is it because she is bored or sleepy, or is it because she is clearly on her method and knows that I have nothing to do with her? This being the first day of retreat, I would guess that it is the former reason.

The third condition is to let go of all thoughts about yourself. When in pain, say to yourself, "I am meditating. These pains have nothing to do with me." Or this sleepy practitioner can tell herself, "My body may be drowsy, but it has nothing to do with me. I will continue my practice."

The same is true of wandering thoughts. Once you realize you are caught in their web, just return to the method. Wandering thoughts are not you. The person who just entertained wandering thoughts is also no longer you. That person is now part of the past. In the present moment, you are working hard on your method. If what I am saying is useful, accept it but do not dwell on it. Likewise, do not imagine what the next moment will bring. You will experience it soon enough.

If you can isolate yourself in this manner—first from the outside, then from those around you, then from your own body and wandering thoughts, and finally from the past and future moments—then you, your method, and the environment will disappear. This is the ideal. When practitioners claim they have reached such a level of absorption, it is usually for a different reason. Usually they have become fatigued from expending so much energy and have fallen into a stupor. Many people who claim to have enlightenment experiences have merely gone blank from exhaustion. Obviously this is not the condition of which the *Song* speaks. If it were, many of you would already be enlightened.

Without seeing there is constant appearance also refers to the enlightened mind. To an enlightened being, all phenomena are still present and moving, but there is no self that interacts with them. This condition is wisdom. There is complete awareness of phenomena and their movements, including the movements of the body, but there is no self that attaches to them. If you get a taste of being undisturbed by the environment, you will feel free and at ease. If you get to the point where your former thought and subsequent thoughts have no relationship to each other, you will feel even freer.

This is not easy to do. Ordinary human beings are moved by thoughts, feelings, and emotions, by concerns of the past and future, by others around them, and by the everyday world. We are also moved by sensations of the body, and if our body is sore, ill, or exhausted, it is difficult to concentrate on meditation. Going on retreat allows us to devote the time and effort necessary to isolate ourselves from such relationships.

On this first day of retreat, begin by isolating yourself from the outside world. Let go of all thoughts about the day you just experienced. For the next seven days, your world is the present moment. Devote all of your attention to it.

10.2 ▪ Practice Starts with Self-Centered Ego

> Completely penetrating everything,
> It has always pervaded everywhere.

When there are neither objects to be seen nor a self who sees them, yet there is still clear and constant awareness, then one is *completely penetrating everything*—all phenomena in all realms of space and time are completely understood. It is difficult to grasp the magnitude of such limitless awareness. Compared to knowing all that exists in all realms, the powers of a psychic are insignificant. Even if there were a truly wise philosopher-king who transformed the lives of all humans, his power would still be limited to planet Earth. Only when there is no longer a self is it possible to have limitless comprehension.

A goal of practice is to reduce the importance of the ego as well as the environment. The smaller the ego, the smaller the obstructions you will have. Conversely, the bigger the ego, the greater the obstructions. We see this all the time. We envy the simplicity of innocent children and those who seem content with very little, yet we strive for power, money, stature, and responsibility. We do this knowing that material wealth and power bring responsibilities and problems.

As we make progress we must check ourselves, lest our egos inflate. Do you become proud and excited? If you use your new insights for your own benefit, your powers will be limited. Therefore ask yourself, "Are my motives selfish or altruistic?"

True Chan practitioners cultivate practice for the sake of other sentient beings. This is what developing bodhi mind means. Such an attitude may seem antagonistic to the ideal of striving to become better, and to develop a strong sense of self. Everywhere people talk about empowerment, about building self-esteem, and confidence. Shelves are lined with self-help books; people listen to tapes, go to lectures, attend workshops, and so on. The logic is sound: if we cannot even help ourselves, if we ourselves are weak, scattered, insecure, powerless, and neurotic, how can we begin to help others?

Even though a goal of practice is to reduce the influence of ego, still it is the ego that decides to do this. We always start from the perspective of self-centered ego. When teaching beginners, I speak of progressing from the sense of scattered small self to a concentrated small self, and then to large universal self, and ultimately to no-self. Notice that on the way to no-self, we must strengthen and consolidate our egos. A side benefit of practice is that we do indeed become more secure, clear, and confident.

The Mahayana way is to start from the position of self in order to move toward no-self for the benefit of sentient beings. That is why the first of the Four Vows is to help others, and the last is to attain supreme enlightenment. Hence, we should always place sentient beings in the forefront of our actions and intentions. Our own vexations often lessen when we give our time and energy to others.

Skeptics may find it hard to believe that one can help even a few people, let alone all sentient beings, but you must start somewhere. You do not have to be perfect to help others. Suppose a group of children want to climb over a high wall, but none of them can do it on his or her own. One of them decides to get down on her hands and knees so that the others can boost themselves over the wall. You can choose to be the one on the bottom. It does not take superior intelligence, skill, or strength to help others. All it takes is motivation.

Are you willing to be the stool for other people, or would your pride and ego suffer too much? Perhaps you prefer someone else to get down on his knees so you can get over the wall. If that is the case, we will change the first vow to, "I vow to let innumerable sentient beings help me." With an attitude like this, one will never experience no-self. You may gain some power from the practice, but it will be limited, and I guarantee your vexations will not lessen. In fact, you will create even larger obstructions and greater vexations. Do you want to bully someone else into helping you over the wall? If so, you are using others to achieve your goal, but what is a wall compared to climbing to the stars? The truth is that the vision of self-serving people is usually as limited as their powers and abilities.

When you do not place importance on your self, everything becomes smoother and easier. When you ultimately reach the stage of no-self, there will be no obstructions whatsoever. There will be no limit to what you can do. Without a self, there is no particular place where you reside. Hence, you are in all places at once. This is freedom without boundaries.

In the beginning it is like being in a locked house with shuttered windows. As you practice you will begin to open doors and windows to let in more light, but still your view is quite limited. Later you step outside and are awed by the vastness of your newly developed vision, but still you can only see up and outward. For the most part the Earth blocks your view. You continue to practice until you transcend the Earth, and like an astronaut, you have an unobstructed view. Even at this point your vision is still limited because you are still a person. There is just so much that you can do and see when you are limited to what you believe to be the self. Ultimately, you must leave the ego behind.

So we begin with the small self; one who sits in a particular place and works hard on a method of practice. Eventually your mind and your method will become smaller and smaller until they disappear. During interview today someone thought they had achieved such a state of absorption. After working diligently for several sitting periods, his energy left him and he felt nothing, or something that he described as blankness. I told him that this was not a case of mind and method disappearing. His experience could be better described as "sitting in a ghost's cave on

Black Mountain." Blankness is similar to being asleep or unconscious. If that is all it takes to experience enlightenment, my job would be much easier. I would just walk behind each one of you and knock you unconscious with a big stick.

It is said that upon attaining great enlightenment, the Buddha saw as many worlds as there were grains of sand in the Ganges River, and knew everything about every sentient being from the past without beginning to the endless future. That is not to say we would gain such all-knowing insight if we were to experience no-self. Experiencing no-self does not necessarily make one a buddha. We may be enlightened to the principle of no-self, but unlike the Buddha, we have not accumulated merit from countless lifetimes of practice.

I was interviewed recently on a Taiwanese radio station. Instead of questions about Buddhism, I was asked questions about love, marriage, family, children, and parents. The interviewer was pleased with my answers, though somewhat surprised by them. He said, "Shifu, I am curious. How is it that you know so much about marriage, love relationships, and family when you left home long ago to become a monk?"

I replied that I base my answers on my experience and knowledge of the principles that underlie all things. By principles I mean those truths and realities that underlie all people, all things, and all dharmas. I may not have personal experience of love or marriage, but the principles that underlie all relationships—all phenomena—are the same.

When you arrive at the place of no people and no seeing, then you too will know how to deal with situations based on your experience of principle. People are troubled and confused because they rely on their limited, self-centered views, because their egos attach to gain and loss. When there is nothing to gain or lose, things get much simpler. Imagine that you are wealthy, and you must choose between your riches or the person you love most. Whether you are ordinary or blessed with super powers, your dilemma will be the same and you will suffer. However, if no self is involved, you can lose either or both without vexation, because there is no attachment to gain or loss. You will simply act in accordance with causes and conditions as they arise.

However, this example is something none of us has to face right now. Before we can make our minds and the environment disappear, we must stop our minds from entertaining wandering thoughts. We do what must be done in this moment.

10.3 ▪ Don't Stir Up Muck

> Thinking brings unclarity,
> Sinking and confusing the spirit.

These two lines are perfect for our practice. As you meditate, do not think about whether or not you are working hard; do not think about whether your method is right for you; do not think about whether the practice is of any use, or if you have a suitable personality for practice. Thoughts like these are hindrances to practice.

Our ordinary mind is not like pure water in a crystal glass; it is more like a murky pond. If the water in the pond is not stirred, it will settle and become clearer and clearer. However, if you feel a need to clear the pond of all the things that might make it cloudy, you will only stir up all the muck that had settled to the bottom. Do not be too curious about what is in the mud. The water was quite clean until you started to stir up the muck.

We do this with wandering thoughts, constantly indulging in or repressing them. If you start chasing every thought that comes up, or searching for the intention that caused such a thought, your mind will never become clear. Examining your thoughts this way only confuses you more.

Every time you meditate, just remind yourself to be diligent, and do not worry about wandering thoughts. This is easier said than done. Every night I give a Dharma lecture that only provides more fodder for you to chew on. People often latch onto a phrase or concept from a sutra, and go over it in their minds while they meditate. Some people have a meditation experience, and then try to find something that they have read that will confirm the experience. Some people listen to my lectures and then try to figure out if my words were meant for them.

Some compare my words to those of the sutras, perhaps to see how closely my understanding accords with the Dharma. These are all incorrect ways to practice and a waste of time.

One of you today complained during interview, "Shifu, you're messing me up. You tell us not to think, and then you give us all this stuff to think about." Is this true for many of you? I apologize, but I will not stop lecturing. You must learn to tame your monkey minds. If I advise someone to get a drink of water, it is of no concern to the rest of you. Do not start wondering if drinking water helps meditation. Likewise, there is no reason for the person to whom I offered water to dwell on the reasons why. Just drink it.

If I teach false Dharma, that is not your problem; the responsibility is mine and I'll be the one who gets bad karma. Some may think, that's easy for Shifu to say, but if he says something false that I accept as true, and then incorporate it into my practice and life, then I may follow him to hell. For this reason, it is important to have faith in what the Buddha taught, and faith that what I teach is in accordance with Buddhadharma. Of course, you don't need faith in me personally to benefit from meditation; but you will get more out it if you trust my guidance.

This morning I told you that you need to have faith in yourself. All buddhas are sentient beings just as you are, and you are also a buddha who has not yet realized it. You must also have faith in the Three Jewels—the Buddha, the Dharma, and the Sangha. This includes me, for I represent the Sangha. Lastly, you need to have faith in your method.

Things are different during retreat. It would be unwise during daily life to neglect thinking about everyday matters. On retreat there is no need to analyze anything. There are three simple rules when you come to meditate: first, no matter what you are doing, be direct; second, no matter what happens, accept it, and once it is past, let it go; third, do not have doubts about the teachings, the method, or yourself.

To repeat, do not waste valuable time dwelling on ideas or doubting yourself. The simpler your mind the better. For philosophers, doctors, artists, and poets, retreats can be a challenge. It is hard for doctors and philosophers to let go of their logic, and it is difficult for artists and poets to put down their imaginations. As a monk I lived for a few years in Japan while I was studying for my doctorate. During retreats, the master would always scold me, saying my intelligence was a hindrance. He was a good teacher who did not allow me to get lost in a world of ideas and logic. Many here are scholars and artists. Do not make me scold you the way my teacher scolded me. While on retreat, make yourselves simple and place all of your attention on your methods. You will return to your ordinary worlds soon enough.

10.4 ▩ Methods Do Not Get Stale, People Do

> Use mind to stop activity
> And it becomes even more erratic.
>
> The ten thousand dharmas are everywhere,
> Yet there is only one door.

Please accept Niutou's advice not to *use mind to stop activity*. If you use the intellect to seek enlightenment, it will only become more confused. If you use the mind to stop vexations and wandering thoughts, it will also become more confused. Either way, you will be unable to develop any power in your practice.

Yes, the ultimate goal of practice is to gain enlightenment. There is also no question that the purpose of meditation is to still the mind. First I tell you that trying to stop the mind to attain enlightenment only causes confusion, and then I say that the goal of practice is to stop the mind. It does not seem to make sense. How can Chan claim to be clear and direct and yet be so confusing?

Experienced practitioners know that before we begin to practice, we need to know why we meditate, but once we begin to meditate, all ideas and goals should be put down. All you should concern yourself with is your method of practice. Your mind is on the present moment, and not comparing experiences to the past or speculating about the future. Yet, this is a big obstacle for many people. They cannot help but use their minds to prevent thoughts from arising, and they get frustrated when it does not work.

The Chinese have many sayings to describe such confusion and misdirected intention. One saying describes an impatient farmer who yanks on rice shoots to make them grow faster. The result is that his impatience uproots the plants and he loses the crop altogether. Another speaks of putting a second head on top of the first one to keep the first one out of trouble. Another maxim speaks of trying to stop water from boiling by pouring hot water into the pot.

The theme that runs through these sayings is that meddling and misdirected intention only complicate things. When it comes to stopping wandering thoughts, we must first remember that the mind is an illusion, albeit a deeply rooted one. We use this illusory mind to transcend the mind of illusion. It is a tricky business. If you try to use your mind to stop your mind from moving, it will not work because the act of trying is moving the mind. On the other hand, if you *allow* your mind to stop moving, it will happen. Every time you try to force your mind to do your bidding, you only serve to create another useless "head" to contend with. Seeking enlightenment in such manner is walking the wrong path.

Using vexation to cure vexation does not work, yet people try it all the time. In fact, psychotherapists make good money attempting to do so. I am not saying that psychological counseling is useless, but its success is often temporary. The best it can do is to replace or cover one illusion with another. It is like trying to stop water from boiling with more hot water. The best thing to do is to put out the fire. Chan methods are devised to help one transcend the mind of vexation by placing one's energy on the practice method and paying no regard to the mind. Since the mind is illusory, there is no need to worry about it. You may not solve your problems, but through meditation your mind will become clearer and more stable. You will recognize your moods and patterns, the way your mind works, and in so doing, eventually discover that your so-called problems have disappeared.

Chan methods seem easy and direct, yet there are far fewer Chan teachers than there are psychologists. Perhaps I should call myself a psychologist and teach people Chan. Once I did a series of radio shows in New York, and at the end of each show people would call in with questions. My advice seemed to be useful, but the truth is, none of the answers came from me. I just passed along information that I received from Chan masters of the past. You may think it's easier to be a Chan master than to be a Chan student, and that students work hard while the master quotes the Buddha and the patriarchs. If you think this way, I can become a therapist, and you can teach Chan. Otherwise it is best for a student to stick to the method and work hard.

In our practice, we do not want our minds to be moved by the environment, whether the thought or feeling is pleasant or unpleasant. Most people are in no hurry to ignore pleasant states of mind. They perceive them to be a beneficial result of practice and attempt to hold on to them. I am sure this has happened to all of you. You will notice, however, that the pleasant condition will slip away as soon as you begin to cling to it. Regret usually follows, and then you look for ways to bring back that good feeling. Before long you are lost in a tangle of wandering thoughts leading to frustration, anger, depression, or self-doubt. After a few moments, minutes, or hours of this, you become fed up and feel like yelling to your mind to stop. That technique does not work. The only thing that works is allowing your mind to return to the method to begin anew.

Telling yourself not to think does not work because that is a thought in itself. Working hard on the method works, but working hard does not mean tensing every muscle, constricting the brain, and spending lots of energy wrapping your mind around the method. I always say, "Relax your body, relax your mind, and work hard." These are not contradictions. If you are tense or struggling, you will eventually run out of energy, become fatigued, and be open to a new flood of wandering thoughts. Working hard means patiently and persistently staying on the method, and immediately returning to it if you find that you have lost it. This takes vigilance and will power, not excessive energy.

When meditating, do not be concerned with any previous experiences, good or bad. If you experienced something pleasant, even a period of clarity, do not try to repeat the steps that you think got you there. If you experienced something unpleasant, do not try to avoid what you think got you in that position. The past is gone; the future has not arrived. All you have is the present moment, which can never be the same as any other moment from the past or future. Therefore, it is pointless to return to what you think was a favorable state of mind. You are different, the environment is different, the moment is different—

everything is different. Even if you repeat an experience, it is a different product of new, interacting causes and conditions. Every moment, your mind should reaffirm the present moment, and the way to do this is to stay on your practice. Any thoughts of the past or future will only cause you to stir up more wandering thoughts.

The lines, *The ten thousand dharmas are everywhere, yet there is only one door,* warn against doubting your method. Practitioners want to feel that they are making progress. They want to know if they can move on to a new, different, or better method. Perhaps they think that a method yields a certain benefit, and once the benefit is gained you discard the method for a better one. It is like standing atop a mountain gazing at another, supposedly higher mountain in the distance, wishing to be there instead. Someone may tell you, "A distant mountain always seems more beautiful than the one you are standing on." No matter—off you go running down one mountain and up another. At the top you feel satisfied, but once again, in the distance you see an even higher peak. So off you go again, thinking it will be the best and last. When you arrive at the top, it is devoid of life and vegetation and you are cold, hungry, and thirsty.

Practitioners are often like a frustrated mountain climber. They think that the method they currently use is inferior and they cannot wait to try another. People who count their breaths wish to work on a *huatou*, people working on one *huatou* feel that another one might be better. Or people reciting mantras wish to practice silent illumination. Once while lecturing in Iowa, I mentioned that the early Chan masters practiced the method of no-method, and that for those who are ready, this is the best practice. After the lecture I was amazed by someone who said to me, "I agree with you that no-method is the best method. Would you teach it to me?"

The best approach is to choose one method and stick with it. Derive as much flavor from it as you can. Continually switching from one method to another, you will never penetrate any of them deeply enough to derive good benefits. Stay with one method and get to the heart of it.

Several people who are using breath counting are anxious to move on to a *huatou* or silent illumination. For some reason they feel that counting breaths is a beginner's method, whereas *huatou* and silent illumination are advanced. There are many paths to no-self, and counting breaths is one of them. It can take you to enlightenment, but that should not be your concern. If you question why you are using one method and not another instead of focusing on the one you have, you are in no position to be seeking a more "advanced" method.

If you truly concentrate on breath counting, the method will eventually disappear. At that point, your method will naturally change to silent illumination. Therefore, do not worry that you may be missing out on something because you are counting your breaths. Besides, there are many variations of and approaches to counting breaths. As people continue to practice, they discover that their understanding of the method evolves. This is one of the qualities of a good, vital meditation method. If you feel it has become stale, come to me and I will help you. The truth is, methods do not become stale, only people do.

If you are having recognizable problems with your method, I consider it a sign of progress. It means that you are working hard. I am more worried about the people who never seem to have problems. Such people sit on their cushions in a happy fog and think it is a clear, enlightened state of mind. Whenever I ask them how they are doing, they look at me with a dreamy smile and say, "Fine." That concerns me. Other people say, "I don't know. I'm not sure if I'm practicing right or not." When I ask them how they are using the method, they respond, "Oh, the way you taught me." I am not a mind reader. I cannot help people if they cannot tell me what they are experiencing. If you have problems or concerns about your practice and you want my help, you must at least meet me halfway. Come with specific questions that I can address.

Most of all do not be lured by stagnant states of mind where nothing is happening and everything seems to be okay. For instance, someone told me yesterday that wandering thoughts always disrupt her concentration at the same point in her meditation. She decided that such an occurrence must be a normal phenomenon and was content to experience it over and over again. Yes, it is normal for wandering thoughts to arise when you practice, but when the same thing happens every time at the same point in your practice, then there is a problem that needs to be investigated. At least this woman was able to recognize it and come to me for guidance.

Her problem reminds me of the time when I was a young man in the army. One of the soldiers was designated to go out every morning to buy food for the troops. With an empty sack slung over his shoulder, he would head out before dawn and walk to the market. One morning, he decided to take a shortcut through a cemetery. He walked and walked for quite some time, and he began to wonder if this was a shortcut after all. Still, he walked and walked, passing gravestone after gravestone. As dawn arrived it became light enough for him to see. It was only then that he realized he had been walking in circles around the cemetery. I hope none of you are circumnavigating graveyards in your mind. If so, you already know the solution—return to the method and leave your mind alone.

10.5 ▪ Meditating in the Boiler Room of the Mind

> Neither entering nor leaving,
> Neither quiet nor noisy.

These lines speak to enlightened beings as well as to beginning practitioners. The *Heart Sutra* states, "This voidness of all dharmas is not born, not destroyed, not impure, not pure, does not increase or decrease." The coming and going of dharmas, of birth and death, of leaving samsara and entering nirvana, are all produced by our discriminating minds.

It is easy to intellectually accept these concepts. "You have vexations? Well, vexations and wisdom are one and the same." "Practice? Why bother? Ignorance is the same as enlightenment, samsara is the same as nirvana, and we are already buddhas." "There is no coming and going, so why worry about birth and death?" These are just rationalizations.

The *Heart Sutra* speaks of the enlightened condition. For ordinary sentient beings with discriminating minds and self-attachment, birth and death *still* exist, vexation and wisdom *are* different, and practice leads one from samsara to nirvana. From the point of view of sentient beings, this is all true. But when one actually leaves behind vexation and attachment to self, one will realize that vexation and wisdom, as well as samsara and nirvana, are one and the same. When there is no more clinging to birth and averting death, then you are in nirvana. But if your mind is still influenced by the environment and you are still governed by karma, you still reside in samsara.

Neither entering nor leaving refers to the deeply enlightened person, but beginners can also use this principle. When you practice, do not avoid wandering thoughts or pain, and do not strive for samadhi or enlightenment; do not seek anything. Just stay with the method. Beginning practitioners can also make use of the line, *Neither quiet nor noisy*. First-time retreatants at the Chan Center are surprised to discover that we are located in the heart of New York City. If you were after peace and quiet, you came to the wrong place. We are bombarded by sounds from outside—traffic, school children, people coming and going to work, buses stopping and starting right outside our doors, not to mention sounds from the inside—phones, people walking, the sounds and smells from the kitchen. If you are moved by these sounds, then it will be difficult to concentrate on your method. But if you attend to your method, then the sounds will not be a bother. Sounds are everywhere; it is you who must adapt.

There was a monk who could not concentrate on his practice for long periods of time. There was just too much noise and commotion for him in the monastery. So he decided to practice alone in the mountains. When he got there he relaxed—finally, no one to disturb his practice. Just as he sat under a tree to meditate, a bird started chirping. He tried to put the chirping out of his mind, but he could not. Trying to chase the bird away was useless. Finally, he thought, "It's the trees that draw the birds, so I'll go where there are no trees." He walked to a meadow and began to meditate again. "Ahh, no more birds." But he forgot about the insects. He would slap the ground and that would quiet them for a few seconds, but they would soon begin again.

After a while it all became unbearable. He thought, "This is not a good place for meditation. Let me go to a place where there are no bugs or birds." He walked until he found a small pond that was fed by a stream. Soon after he sat down, the frogs started to croak, and behind that noise he could hear the continual trickle of the stream. He realized that there was no place that was quiet, and decided to take matters into his own hands. He balled up small pieces of cloth and stuck them in his ears. Now it did not matter where he sat because he could not hear anything. "Now I'll be able to meditate," he thought.

He sat for a few minutes, when suddenly, "Where is the sound of drums coming from?" When he removed the cloth to listen, the drumming stopped. As soon as he put the cloth back in his ears, the drumming resumed. Then he realized the drumming was the sound of his own beating heart. Disgusted, the monk figured, "I'm just not cut out for meditation. I may as well forget it." Later on, a master told him, "Your problem is not the sounds, but your mind that is moved by sounds." On hearing those words the monk was enlightened.

This is good advice for all of us. In and of themselves phenomena cannot disturb you. It is the mind that is moved by phenomena, and calling them disturbances. I hope that you can put this into practice, especially those of you sitting on the street side. However, if you are like this monk and find outside sounds a distraction, we can always move you and your cushion to the boiler room.

The wisdom of sravakas and pratyekabuddhas

11.1 ▩ Hinayana and Mahayana

> The wisdom of sravakas and
>   pratyekabuddhas
> Cannot explain it.

These lines assert that the wisdom of a bodhisattva goes beyond that of a *sravaka* or a *pratyekabuddha*. In Sanskrit, the word *sravaka* means "hearer," and originally referred to a disciple of the Buddha. In Mahayana Buddhism the term more specifically refers to one who seeks personal enlightenment through the Four Noble Truths. The goal of a *sravaka* is to leave the cycle of birth and death (samsara) and enter nirvana, that is, to become an arhat. In Sanskrit, *pratyekabuddha* means a "solitary enlightened one" who has attained enlightenment without having encountered the Buddhadharma. Such a person has achieved this by understanding the "twelve links of conditioned arising" as a result of causes and conditions. This enlightenment is higher than that of a *sravaka* or *arhat*, but is not the complete enlightenment of a buddha.

In mentioning *sravakas* and *pratyekabuddhas*, Niutou refers to practitioners of the Hinayana path. The original adherents of the Mahayana school believed that the Hinayana path emphasized self-liberation as the goal of practice, while the Mahayana path emphasized the bodhisattva ideal of saving sentient beings. How these two schools compare is not relevant to our practice. I am just offering some background to better explain these verses.

In the *sravaka* path, even when in samadhi that gives rise to wisdom, one cannot and does not interact with others. This neither harms others nor helps them. On the other hand, although free from vexation, enlightened bodhisattvas still interact with and help others. In this sense the enlightenment of a *sravaka* who practices for self-liberation is not comparable to that of a bodhisattva who practices for the sake of sentient beings.

There are three aspects to practicing Buddhism: precepts or morality (*sila*), meditation (*samadhi*), and wisdom (*prajna*). Following the precepts is practicing Buddhadharma in daily life and reducing self-centeredness. Samadhi, or deep concentration, is the result of practicing meditation in a diligent manner. In cultivating deep samadhi, one's mind and being will eventually be transformed to reveal wisdom.

Both schools of Buddhism agree that the three aspects of practice are a natural progression on the path. However, the Mahayana school says that through diligent practice, one can go directly from practicing precepts to experiencing wisdom. That is precisely the goal of the *huatou* practice of Chan. Therefore, while the two schools have the same foundations of morality, meditation, and wisdom, their purposes and their methods differ.

For instance, in both schools mindfulness of the breath is one of the five methods for stilling the mind. As such, counting breaths is excellent for stabilizing the mind and body and for reducing wandering thoughts. According to Hinayana philosophy, however, counting breaths is not sufficient for entering samadhi, let alone attaining wisdom. After practicing one of the five methods, one must then attain three deeper levels of absorption before entering samadhi.

The Hinayana teaching is that wisdom must follow samadhi, but Chan teaches that the purpose of practice is not to enter samadhi, but to experience wisdom directly. Still, I strongly advocate counting breaths as a practice method because it is an excellent method for concentrating the mind. In Chan you still practice counting the breath to become more concentrated, but when your mind is free of most wandering thoughts, you are better positioned to use a *huatou* to arouse the "great mass of doubt." Through diligent practice, when your mass of doubt reaches a climax and dissolves, you may then experience sudden enlightenment. Thus, in Chan it is possible to experience wisdom without going through samadhi.

It is unlikely that anyone here will reach that level of practice on this first day of retreat. In fact it is rare to reach it even after several intensive retreats. So, any intention you have of arousing and dissolving a great mass of doubt will only obstruct you. The initial purpose is to calm and stabilize your mind so it will no longer be so wild and scattered. At that point pain, numbness, and itching will not distract your attention, and neither will any passing moods or emotions.

The appropriate time to use a *gong'an* or a *huatou* is when your mind is under control. *Gong'ans* are stories about enlightenment experiences of past masters and patriarchs, or encounters between a master and a disciple. A *huatou* is typically a single phrase, such as "Who am I?" which a practitioner uses to investigate the meaning of the particular *gong'an*. "Investigate" means trying to find the answer to the question posed without resorting to concepts and reasoning, or even the Buddhist teachings. Usually one is told to ignore whatever arises in the mind, for that will not be the answer. One just continues to ask the question in a concentrated, earnest manner. Eventually a doubt sensation will rise and it will grow until it becomes an all-encompassing mass of doubt. Typically a practitioner immersed in a great ball of doubt is oblivious to everything but the *gong'an* or *huatou*.

Hopefully, at one point the doubt mass will burst, but this does not always happen. Sometimes one loses energy and the doubt sensation subsides. Investigating a *huatou* is like inflating a balloon. The more air you blow into a balloon the bigger it becomes, just as the doubt sensation will increase when you apply energy to the *huatou*. The hope is to inflate the balloon (the doubt sensation) to the breaking point. Sometimes a balloon has a leak and deflates. In the same way, it may be too difficult to maintain the energy required to penetrate the *huatou*, so the doubt sensation subsides.

Some people may experience a breakthrough in one seven-day retreat. Others work on *huatou* for years before giving rise to the doubt sensation. Chan master Laiguo worked on a single *huatou* for years. As a monk he traveled from one place to another with a few provisions in a bag. If he came upon a monastery he would stay for a day or two before moving on. If he found no shelter, he would sit under a tree. If he was hungry and met people, he would ask for food. If he did not meet anyone, it did not matter. The only constant in Laiguo's life was his dedication to investigating the *huatou*. He was immersed in a mass of doubt wherever he went. This went on for years. One day he put down his bag to rest, and his mass of doubt dissolved, resulting in a deep enlightenment experience.

Some people are impatient to investigate a *huatou* before their minds are even concentrated. Using the *huatou* this way will not generate doubt. It will be more like reciting a mantra, but not being a true mantra, it will be dry and meaningless. One would be better off counting breaths, or reciting the Buddha's name. To concentrate the mind initially, counting breaths is much more efficient than *huatou*. Hence we often begin with breath counting before investigating a *huatou*. Hopefully the mind will give rise to the doubt sensation; when that dissolves, wisdom may manifest.

11.2 ▣ Wonderful Wisdom

> Actually there is not a single thing;
> Only wonderful wisdom exists.

First, the *Song* says that *there is not a single thing*, then it says that *wonderful wisdom exists*. How can this be? If nothing exists, then wisdom must not exist either. On the other hand, if wisdom exists, that refutes the notion that nothing exists. There seems to be more here than meets the eye. According to the Mahayana teachings, there are three kinds of nonexistence: that which ordinary sentient beings perceive, that which arhats and *pratyekabuddhas* perceive, and that which bodhisattvas and buddhas perceive.

For sentient beings, "nonexistence" is a relative term used to compare to things that do exist. It is purely conceptual because sentient beings cannot directly experience nonexistence. A poor man may claim that money does not exist for him, but if he dwells on money, then money does exist in his mind. Hence the nonexistence of ordinary sentient beings is as illusory as what they perceive to be real.

The nonexistence that arhats experience is absolute. They have no more vexations or attachments; they have entered nirvana and will not return to samsara. Therefore for arhats, "wonderful wisdom" also does not exist. This is impossible for us to truly comprehend because we perceive things only from the point of view of sentient beings. Hinayana practitioners penetrate deeper and deeper levels of samadhi until they enter nirvana. We perceive this to be a karmic consequence of their intentions and actions. But for arhats who have attained nirvana, space, time, and vexations are absolutely nonexistent.

Therefore, the nonexistence that the verse speaks of is what bodhisattvas perceive. Bodhisattvas have nothing in their minds—no attachments, no vexations, no idea of sentient beings to save, and no bodhisattvas to save them—yet they remain in the world to help. Wonderful wisdom is precisely the bodhisattvas' natural and spontaneous responses to the needs of sentient beings. This wisdom is wonderful because it manifests in whatever form necessary to serve sentient beings.

How do these profound ideas relate to us? To make good use of this retreat, it is important to practice as if nothing else exists except your method. The outside world does not exist; others do not exist. There is no such thing as pain, sleepiness, or boredom. There is no past, no future, and no enlightenment. There is not even you. All that exists is your practice, and that too should eventually disappear.

If you think you have failed so far to clear your mind of wandering thoughts, forget about it. They do not exist. If you think you have sat well today, forget about it. That does not exist either. If you can let go of everything except the method, including yourself, then I guarantee you will experience enlightenment. But I would not dwell on that idea either. While you are practicing, enlightenment should not exist. Once you are enlightened, enlightenment will also not exist. Therefore ignore everything, including what I have just said.

11.3 ▓ What Is the Original Face?

> The original face is limitless;
> It cannot be probed by mind.

Whatever can be known, understood, or conceived is limited. The "mind" that these lines refer to is the discriminating mind, not the undefiled mind of enlightenment. When you meditate for long periods, you are probably amazed at what you remember. It is like watching movies unfolding in your mind. Some of these might actually be movies you have seen. One of my students not only recalls entire movies during retreats but also the previews and the credits. He knows it is a waste of valuable retreat time, but confesses that he wished his memory could be that keen during daily life. Everything else that runs through your mind while you meditate—memories of past events, plans, and visions for the future, fantasies—are also movies unfolding in your mind's eye.

It might seem amazing that you can recall so much information, but is it really that much? Can you even remember everything you thought, said, and did in one twenty-four hour period? As the *Song* implies, the ordinary mind of sentient beings is limited. Imagine for a moment that you could remember everything you ever experienced in your entire life, from the moment you were born until now. Such a feat, if it were possible, would be considered superhuman. Yet even that would be limited, for your mind could not remember everything from previous births since time without beginning. And I am only speaking about you. Could you also be aware of all phenomena of all sentient beings in all worlds from all times?

Obviously, our discriminating minds are far too limited to comprehend even the tiniest fraction of the myriad phenomena that have existed, do exist, and will exist in the infinite worlds of the universe. This totality is precisely the "original face" that the Song mentions. It is true reality, free of attachments, discriminations, and vexations. The totality of the original face includes all times, spaces, and phenomena. However, there is no specific place or time that one can point to and say, "there is the original face."

This limitlessness of the original face is difficult to comprehend. Everything we know, however fleeting or enduring, exists in a particular location and time. For example, can we say the Chan Center houses the original face? Not too long ago the Chan Center was a five-and-dime store. Before that it might have been a house, or a farm, or an empty field.

Twenty thousand years ago it may have been under several hundred feet of glacier, and before that it might have been part of a great sea. Who can say how long this building will remain as the Chan Center? The old center across the street is now a Seventh-day Adventist church. Perhaps the Chan Center will close down when I retire, but even if it continued under the guidance of other sangha members, how long would it last? One generation, perhaps two. Inevitably it will become something else, or the building will get torn down. Obviously, this Chan Center is not the home of the limitless original face.

A few days ago I looked at some recent photos of myself. Under a pile of papers I found photos of me from ten and twenty years ago. I looked better in those. I later gazed at my reflection in the bathroom mirror. Tell me, can any of these images be my original face? No, the body—its physicality—is not the original face. Anything that constantly changes is not the original face.

When I traveled to China, I visited the underground palace of China's first emperor, Qin Shi Huang, which houses thousands of life-sized, terra-cotta soldiers. It is a testament to human ingenuity that this palace still stands, relatively untouched, after twenty-two hundred years. However, the pillars that had once been solid wood had disappeared from long years of decomposition. Eventually the soldiers will return to dust. Mountains will form and erode. Valleys will become oceans and seas will become deserts. None of these things can be considered the original face.

No one thing is the original face, yet the original face encompasses everything. Not even the four elements—earth, fire, water, and air—are the original face, because they too change. Buddhadharma says that the four elements are the medium through which sentient beings receive karmic retribution. Furthermore, our physical form could not exist without the four elements, and we could not create new karma if we didn't interact with them. Nonetheless, the physical realm is not the original face.

If the physical realm is not the original face then perhaps the mind is. But which mind is the original face? The *Song* already stated that the original face cannot be probed by the mind of distinction, so obviously the ordinary mind of sentient beings is not the original face. Karma is also not the original face because karma is forever changing. We receive karmic retribution for our past actions, and in so doing we create new karma. We do so because we cannot help it. As long as we cling to an idea of a self, then our thoughts, words, and actions create karma. This has been so since before the beginning of time.

The truth is that we cannot know this original face with our minds. People who have experienced it cannot describe or point to it. Enlightened beings are not tongue-tied idiots. They know how to communicate, but they also know that it is impossible to describe the original face, because it is not something that can be known by the mind. Obviously, if something can be described or identified, then it can be probed by the mind. I would also add that the original face cannot be known by the intuitive mind either. Many people mistakenly equate the intuitive mind with the enlightened mind. The intuitive mind is a kind of direct, spontaneous knowing, but it still incorporates an individual's point of view and experiences. Therefore, it still derives from a mind of discrimination, attachment, and vexation. It can err, and it is limited.

Hence, we practice to shatter all vexations and obstructions in our minds. Only then will the original face be revealed. The goal of practice is to put down all attachments and self-centeredness, because they are not in accordance with wisdom. Do not ask me what the original face looks like or what enlightenment is. I am not enlightened, and if I were, I could not describe it to you, because enlightenment is beyond the limits of the discriminating mind. Anything I can possibly say about enlightenment would be inaccurate. Even if I could describe enlightenment in detail, what purpose would it serve for you? I can show you a picture of Mount Everest and describe it in detail, but if you want to experience Mount Everest, you must climb it yourself. The best I or any other teacher can do is point the way.

Last night I told you that nothing, including enlightenment, should exist except your practice. Tonight I add that the original face also does not exist while you are practicing. If you practice with the intent of finding it, you will only get lost and frustrated in your own hall of mirrors. There is no need to add to the obstructions you already face.

11.4 ▪ True Enlightenment Is No Enlightenment

> True enlightenment is no enlightenment,
> Real emptiness is not empty.

I have said many times: do not seek enlightenment when you come to retreat. I also say that there is no buddha, so do not try to become one. This sounds crazy—I am sitting in front of a Buddha statue to which we prostrate twice daily, telling you there is no buddha. Every night we talk about enlightenment in the *Song*, and now it says *true enlightenment is no enlightenment*.

When we study the Dharma, it is perfectly fine to think about enlightenment and the Buddha, but while we are practicing, there should be no thoughts about these things. We should not think of the Buddha as some entity outside of ourselves that we wish to be like. When we prostrate we should not seek the Buddha's help. With such thoughts we will not be able to see the Buddha at all. Why then do we prostrate? We prostrate because we are grateful for the Dharma that the Buddha gave us. Without it we would not know how to practice. However, when we prostrate, the only thoughts we should have are of our movements.

Make no mistake—when we prostrate, hold morning and evening services, read sutras, or meditate, we are trying to be *like* the Buddha. We should express gratitude toward this great being. The Buddha does exist, but the Buddha cannot give us enlightenment. Therefore we practice for the sake of practice. Some of you came a long way to sit for seven days. Did you know that you spent all this money and came all this distance to practice just for the sake of practice?

You may ask, "If I continue to sit, won't I get enlightened?" The answer is yes and no. Yes, you will eventually get enlightened, but once you are enlightened, there is no enlightenment. The same is true for buddhahood. I will offer a crude analogy: we can all agree that the Chan Center exists. It exists in our minds, but it also exists as a building in Elmhurst, New York. Before you came, the Chan Center was already here. But once you are in the Center, it no longer exists. Do you understand? If you say it still exists, show it to me. You may point to the wall, to the statues, to the rugs, to the kitchen, even to me, but none of those things is the Chan Center. When you are not here, the Chan Center is a numbered building on a street in a borough of New York City, but once you are inside, it disappears. Those who have become buddhas are inside the building of buddhahood, so to speak, and for them there is no such thing as buddhahood. For those who are outside, however, there is buddhahood. As long as we are outsiders we should follow the Buddha's example and teachings, but we should not strive to be like, or demand anything, from the Buddha.

Real Emptiness Is Not Empty

The second line of this stanza says, *Real emptiness is not empty*. The other day I talked about how a poor person may not have money in his pockets, but his mind is full of it. On the other hand, if all the wealth and money belonged to a single person, would she constantly think of having money? I heard that some immensely wealthy people do not carry any money with them. The reason is that no matter where they go, something is there for them. Even though they are without a cent in their pockets, can we say that these people have no money?

According to their vows, monks and nuns do not own anything, yet they should take care of and cherish everything they use. Wherever they lay their heads is their home, and they take care of it as if it were their home. Even if a nun's home for the night happens to be under a tree, she takes good care of it and leaves it better than she found it. She does this because of her vows and her practice, not for her future benefit, thinking, "since I will be passing this way again, I'll tidy it up for my next visit." She also does not do it for the approval of others. Whomever a monk meets are his friends and relatives; and whatever happens to him are his affairs. But when he leaves he does not take the people and events with him; they are already past and gone.

We can all benefit by cultivating such an attitude. Because you claim nothing as your own, everything becomes yours; and because everything is yours you have a great responsibility to take good care of it. This is how sincere Chan practitioners should conduct themselves. This is natural behavior for enlightened beings, but not being enlightened, we must train ourselves.

This inner training has nothing to do with outer forms. Most of you are not monastics, yet you can all cultivate this attitude. It is not a behavior reserved only for members of the monastic sangha. Do not mistake outer forms for inner training. Outer forms have nothing to do with practice. The Buddha is often depicted sitting on a lotus blossom. Does that mean you have to meditate on a lotus blossom too? Perhaps you are thinking you ought to get robes like the Buddha, and his hair is so lovely the way it curls around his head. Maybe you should get your hair done that way. You may laugh, but we have all done something similar at one time or another.

While I was in China, I visited an ancient Buddhist site that had been turned into a tourist attraction. The site dated from the Tang dynasty, and they had replicas of clothing from that time period. People could dress up like Tang monks and be photographed so they had something to show their friends and family when they returned home. I was standing off to the side, watching, and people would say, "Oh, look! A real monk!" Wearing the robes of a monk or nun does not automatically make someone spiritually better. Imitation may be a form of flattery, but we should imitate the Buddha by transforming our minds, not our externals. Plant the seed by following the teachings of the Buddha and emulating the bodhisattvas.

With true emptiness there is nothing to seek and nothing to attain. Anything we seek or wish to attain is therefore just another wandering thought. Concentrate totally in the present moment. On every retreat, I say the same thing: practice itself is the goal. You will benefit most if you have this attitude. When a farmer plants a fruit tree, he does not expect to immediately harvest ripe fruit. He knows of the tree's potential, but he cares for it in the present moment, whether it has fruit or not. Do not concern yourself with the fruits of practice. There is only the process.

11.5 ▦ Stepping Closer to Your Own Enlightenment

> All buddhas of the past, present and future
> All ride on this basic principle.

The *basic principle* recalls the previous stanza, which says that once you are enlightened, or are inside enlightenment, so to speak, there is no enlightenment to attain. All vexations and all attachments are gone. That is not to say that nothing exists. True emptiness is true existence, but only if you can experience true emptiness will you know what true existence is. Buddhas are buddhas because they *ride on*, or are in accordance with, this principle.

When the *Heart Sutra* speaks of "all the buddhas of the past, present, and future," it may seem as if it is talking about beings who have nothing to do with us. But actually we are included in this group, and we represent the buddhas of the future. Shakyamuni, Amitabha, and several other buddhas mentioned in sutras are buddhas of the present era. In fact, there are innumerable buddhas of the present presiding over innumerable worlds. If they were buddhas of the past, we would know nothing about them. Shakyamuni is a buddha who resides in this world and time and whose teachings still touch us. Sutras say that in this *kalpa*, an unimaginably long period of time, there will be thousands of buddhas who will appear, and Shakyamuni was just the third in this long list. According to the sutras, Maitreya will be the next buddha, and sometime in the remote future all of us will also be buddhas.

If you wish to visit buddhas of other worlds and times, I suggest you start saving up for that journey now because it is a long and costly trip. On the other hand, there really is no need to go anywhere. We are already blessed because Shakyamuni is right here and now in our world. If you are going to plan for anything, let it be for your own buddhahood, even if it is a hundred trillion years from now. Every time you sit in clear awareness you have stepped a little closer toward enlightenment.

All who have encountered Buddhadharma have already planted seeds for their future buddhahood. In fact, people who oppose Buddhism have also planted seeds for their future buddhahood. Sutras say that anyone who slanders the Buddha or the Dharma will spend time in hell. When they realize why they are in hell, perhaps they will reconsider and change their minds about Buddhadharma. I have told the story of a Song dynasty official who hated Buddhism and wished to discredit it in a scathing treatise entitled *The Nonexistence of the Buddha*.

For months he wracked his brains trying to refute Buddhism. Finally his wife suggested that he study the sutras and *shastras* so that he could better organize his own ideas and feelings. He agreed, and began to study the sutras. Eventually he had a change of heart and became a great lay practitioner.

People who accept and practice the Dharma have chosen a direct route to buddhahood, while people who oppose it have chosen an indirect route. Nonetheless, all are on their way. The ones who have not yet found the path are those who do not care at all about the Dharma, and those who know nothing of it. Even so, this can change in an instant if they open their minds and hearts to the teachings of the Buddha, in this or any other world and time.

Conditions for Progress

For Chan practitioners, contemplating how to plant the seeds for their future buddhahood has nothing to do with being aware in the present moment. To ensure your future buddhahood just take care of the present moment, and do not worry about how well or poorly you are doing. All great masters throughout history followed a similar path, fulfilling four conditions: they made great vows, had great faith, had great determination, and generated great doubt.

We can walk the same path by meeting the four conditions. First, make vows that will strengthen your faith, determination, and will. The Four Great Vows are a great place to start, but you can also make individual vows that will help to strengthen your practice. Second, develop great faith in the Dharma, in the teacher or teachers you decide to follow, in your method of practice, and, most importantly, in yourself. Third, with great faith and the power generated by your vows, you will cultivate great determination in your practice, and eventually this determination will give rise to the fourth condition, great doubt.

Some of you have said that you feel hypocritical making vows you cannot keep. Do not be disheartened. For many of us the Four Great Vows are unimaginable in their depth and meaning. Nonetheless, you should take these vows because they plant seeds that will someday sprout. Vows help to make your practice stronger. Do not despair if you cannot keep even your own individual vows. Each time you approach your cushion, bow to it and make a vow: "I will not be moved by pain; I will not be overcome by sleepiness; I will not get lost in wandering thoughts." Make these vows with sincerity, then forget them. Have faith that the seeds planted by these vows are within you, and then put your mind on the task at hand, your method. If you are overwhelmed by pain, do what you must, but if you move, do it with the same sincerity you used when making the vow. When the sitting is over, do not chastise yourself for breaking a vow. This is the process. Next time you sit, make the same vow again. In this way you will slowly but surely strengthen your determination.

People are forever missing the point: it is precisely because you cannot always keep your vows that you keep making them. If you could meditate for hours without being moved by pain, drowsiness, or wandering thoughts, then there is no point in making a vow about such things. All buddhas of the past and present followed the same path, making vows over and over until they accomplished their goals.

People are often confused, thinking that being determined is at odds with being relaxed. Determination does not mean being tense and coiled like a tight spring; it means being patiently persistent in your approach to the method. When you find yourself off the method, bring yourself back, but do so in a gentle and relaxed way. Tension will lead to exhaustion and other obstructions. That is why I always say, relax your body and mind, and work hard.

What is your strategy when you climb a mountain? Are you going to treat it like a hundred-yard dash and start sprinting up the mountainside? I guarantee you will not get very far. Better to walk at a slow and steady pace and plan on camping overnight a few times. But once you begin, you should not dwell on thoughts about what you might experience when you reach the top. Once you begin, your mind is on one foot in front of the next. Meditating is like climbing that tall mountain. Do not worry about anything but your own method. Do not compare yourself to others. You have your pace and others have their pace. You have no idea what they are experiencing, and it is no concern of yours. Just use great determination to keep your mind on your affairs.

Once there was a Chan monk who was plagued by drowsiness. He would forever find himself nodding off on the cushion. He decided on a risky strategy, and sat at the edge of a cliff. "If I doze off, I will fall to my death. That will keep me alert," he thought. Nevertheless, he got sleepier and sleepier until finally, he dozed off and fell off the cliff. As he was falling, he awoke and instantly got enlightened. Then he realized that he was still sitting at the top of the cliff. If you wish to use this technique, you can sit on the third-floor windowsill. How sincere and determined are you? Will you want a safety net?

World in a Grain of Sand

> The tip of a hair of this basic principle
> Contains worlds numerous as the Ganges sands.

The tip of a hair is a phrase often used in Buddhist sutras and texts. In this case it means that the enlightened mind is so vast that even the tiniest fraction of such a mind contains as many worlds as the Ganges sands. A few years ago I was interviewed by a reporter for a New York radio station. The New York marathon was under way at the same time. I said that from the Chan point of view, all the people in New York could run a marathon race on a single grain of sand. He asked how this could be so, and I explained that running a marathon on a grain of sand is possible if we do so with our limitless minds, a mind with no attachments or vexations. This is because our minds do not occupy space. Though its size is limitlessly vast, no part of it occupies any space or time.

In Chan practice, your method might be to take an entire hour to walk from one side of a grain of sand to the other. If you could do this without losing concentration, so that there were no gaps between your intended thoughts, you would enter samadhi before the hour was over. Could you maintain that concentrated awareness, or would you grow bored? Would you flick that boring sand grain out of your mind and ask for something more interesting on which to meditate? Perhaps you would prefer instead to walk across a strand of hair. It does not matter. If you are wholly and continuously focused on the method of traversing across those objects, then a strand of hair can be longer than the Golden Gate Bridge and a grain of sand can be vaster than Earth. Practitioners can use such methods before enlightenment, and if they succeed, they will discover how something exceedingly small can become exceedingly large.

What the *Song* refers to, however, is what occurs after enlightenment. When there are no more attachments and discriminations, there are no more ideas of small and large. The enlightened mind is beyond all descriptions and comparisons. Hence, it contains all things. These lines describe deeply enlightened states of mind, but how can we use them to help us in our daily lives? On our way to becoming a buddha, we can make our character better accord with wisdom and compassion. It is said that with true love there cannot be a third person. This speaks of a restrictive and possessive kind of love that is not even compassion. Perhaps if your mind and heart were to widen and become more accepting, you would be able to love many people, but this is still not the unlimited mind.

A Chinese proverb says that a brave person puts fear into the hearts of his enemies, while a wise person embraces everyone. The greatest generals in ancient times did not fight wars, yet entire enemy armies surrendered to them.

As practitioners we wish to cultivate compassionate minds, to become more accepting of ourselves and of others. We may not have the limitless capabilities of the Buddha and bodhisattvas, but we can at least work in that direction. In so doing, our minds and hearts will expand while compassion and wisdom will grow. Everyone *can* become a buddha, but right now we are still ordinary sentient beings. If we cannot learn to become kind and considerate to people around us, practicing meditation is pointless. Buddhism is not interested in debating whether some people are good or bad, or whether the nature of humans is good or evil. Buddhadharma desires to improve the human character through practice.

The Buddha is not an alien being; he is a model among human beings, something we can all aspire to. That is why we practice.

We begin by gathering our small, scattered minds into sound, healthy, concentrated minds. This itself is a great accomplishment. If people could arrive even at this level, all of humanity would be transformed. Next, we move beyond unification of attention to unification of body and mind. Normally we are moved by problems of the mind or body, but if we can achieve the state where thoughts are cut off, then all problems will disappear. Beyond unity of body and mind is unity of the "I" and the environment. At this level we recognize that all things, affairs, and people are not different or separate from us. At this level the heart naturally gives rise to compassion, which is beyond the limits of sympathy and conditional love.

If you cannot experience the unification of the "I" and the environment, you will not be truly compassionate in the Buddhist sense. This does not mean that ordinary compassion is worthless; you do the best you can. But if you sincerely want to improve your character according to Buddhadharma, then you must take appropriate measures. For practitioners that means staying focused on your method, so that you can begin calming and collecting your scattered mind. All the education and social training in the world does not compare to doing the work directly. Chan is direct; it asks you to put aside theories and speculations and face yourself, because only by facing yourself can you develop a sound and healthy character.

Do not concern yourself
with anything

12.1 ■ No Concern with Past or Future

> Do not concern yourself with anything;
> Fix the mind nowhere.
> Fixing the mind nowhere,
> Limitless brightness shows itself.

To make good use of your time on this retreat, heed the first line in this stanza, and *do not concern yourself with anything*. First, do not concern yourself with the past and future, what you did before you came, and what you expect to do afterwards. Second, do not concern yourself with anything that happens around you during this retreat. You may hear cars, buses, and radios, but they have nothing to do with you. You may also witness people around you making noises, crying, laughing, or moving around; this is not your concern either. If you pay attention to external phenomena, you will not be able to focus on your practice. Third, do not concern yourself with your previous or next thoughts. If you can do these three things, I guarantee that this retreat will be a success for you.

Two obstructions that plague meditators are sleepiness and wandering thoughts. If you are sleepy, use your mind power to overcome the feeling. You can also open your eyes so wide that tears begin to flow. This sometimes dispels drowsiness. If this does not work, you can ask for the incense board. Raise your hand, and either a timekeeper or I will strike you on your shoulders with the flat side of the board. It does not hurt, and it may revive your energy and awareness. If the incense board does not work, you can kneel on the carpet or the floor. You will either stay awake to maintain your balance; or the pain in your knees ought to replace the sleepiness. You can also get up and prostrate for a while. This way your body is moving but you are still focusing your mind. If none of these methods work, it means that you are truly sleepy, and it is best to take a nap in order to refresh your mind and renew your energy.

Wandering thoughts are almost always about the past and future. If you can put down the past and future, then wandering thoughts will not be a problem. However, this is easier said than done. One expedient way to deal with wandering thoughts is to focus on your pain. Even people who are able to sit comfortably for a long time can have difficulty with wandering thoughts. As with sleepiness, you can also kneel on the floor and the discomfort will force you to concentrate.

If you do not feel any obstacles when practicing, it probably means that you are at a standstill. Not that pain and obstacles are requirements for practice—there is no need to seek them out. But they will come, and they are a sign that you are making progress. If you never had any difficulties or obstructions, I would be concerned.

People expect and desire good experiences; at the same time, they resent and wish to avoid bad ones. This attitude does not befit Chan practitioners, who should cultivate equanimity—neither craving good experiences, nor avoiding bad ones. Do not dwell on good or bad memories from the past either. If you had a good sitting, do not waste time congratulating yourself. Also, do not waste time trying to repeat a good experience—it is over. By the same token, do not waste time feeling bad over a poor sitting—it too is over. Just concentrate on the present moment.

It is normal for good and bad things to happen during retreats. It is rare that someone will have seven full days of nothing but joy or misery. People who have meditated for twenty years still have bad sittings. They should not think, "I have wasted all those years because I just had a bad sitting." Even if the entire day was spent grappling with pain, sleepiness, and a scattered mind, it does not matter. That was then, this is now. Regardless of how you felt up to now, your attitude now should be, "It was fine, but now it's over. Where is my method?"

Fixing the Mind Nowhere

Fix the mind nowhere can also be understood as, "when the mind is at perfect rest, there is no place where it abides." This describes the enlightened mind, which is at peace because it attaches to nothing, yet is aware of everything. We, on the other hand, are not enlightened, so we should fix our minds on our method. But do so in a relaxed manner, for a tense mind will not be able to focus on anything for long.

Resting the body and mind should be easy, but for many it is difficult. You rest your mind by letting go of the three things I said earlier: thoughts of your daily life in the past and future, the environment around you, and your previous and successive thoughts. When meditating, your mind is on the method. When doing walking meditation, prostrations, or stretching exercises, your mind is on your movements. When reciting the morning and evening services, your mind is on the sound of your voice. When eating or working, your mind is on the task at hand. Simple enough, yet so many people struggle.

If every second you can focus without any wandering thoughts, you will soon forget about your body. You may become so clear and relaxed that you no longer need your method. At that point, you are approaching the level of *fixing the mind nowhere*. But as long as you have the idea that there is no need to fix your mind anywhere, your mind is fixed on that idea. So you must forget that too. When the mind does not fix anywhere, then "limitless brightness" reveals itself; when the mind does not attach to anything, then wisdom naturally arises. This wisdom is also called "empty illumination." Wisdom arises effortlessly when there is no longer a self that discriminates and has vexations. The enlightened person does not feel he or she has any wisdom, yet it is there.

I am often asked, "Are you enlightened?"

My answer is always the same, "No, I am not enlightened." That is the truth. It seems, however, that people do not believe me.

They further ask, "But you must have had some kind of enlightenment experience during your practice. What was it?"

So I try to describe to them what I experienced, and they say, "That doesn't sound like a big deal. I wouldn't call that enlightenment."

At that point I usually reply, "That's right. I already told you I wasn't enlightened."

Then they are a bit confused, perhaps even annoyed. They ask, "Then why do you call yourself a Chan master?"

I answer, "I have never called myself a Chan master. It is others who call me that."

"Then why do you write so many books about Buddhism?" they ask.

"Because I wish to help people. But the words are not mine. I am just passing along what I have learned from the great masters and patriarchs of the past. None of those ideas are mine."

Still, incredulous, they ask, "So, is your mind not always smooth and clear and unattached from all vexations?"

"No," I answer, "I have my ups and downs, my vexations and attachments, just like everyone else. Perhaps mine aren't as burdensome as those of other people, but I still experience frustrations, emotions, and obstructions. I am not enlightened, therefore I still have attachments."

If someone claims to be enlightened, it is a sure sign that they are not. After all, who is it that claims to be enlightened? It is an ego that attaches to such ideas. Like the Buddha, the enlightened still act like human beings and engage in normal activities, but have no attachment to what they do, or what happens to them. They have no need to claim anything. Wisdom and compassion flow naturally from them.

I hope you did not come expecting to sit at the feet of an enlightened master. I am a monk who happens to be guiding an intensive Chan retreat because I have extensive experience in this area. Please make use of these four lines of verse. They encourage us to put down all thoughts, including the erroneous thought that your shifu might be enlightened. It is pointless to dwell on such matters. Do not concern yourself with anyone's enlightenment, including your own. Just fix your mind on your method and let go of the rest.

12.2 ▪ Leave Behind the Seeking Mind

> Tranquil and non-arising,
> Set free in boundless time and space.

Whatever it does, there is no obstruction.
Going and staying are equal.

The first two lines of this stanza describe enlightened mind. If the mind were only tranquil and non-arising, it would not necessarily indicate enlightenment. It is the line, *Set free in boundless time and space*, that truly describes the liberated mind. When there are no attachments and no vexations, the mind is free and limitless. Whatever arises, the mind remains tranquil and non-arising. It responds to others not with discrimination and vexation, but with wisdom and compassion.

Some meditators experience a period in which they have no wandering thoughts, and assume they have discovered Chan wisdom, that they have become enlightened. In fact, abiding in a peaceful state with no thoughts is dwelling in a cocoon of nothingness. It is like the turtle tucking its head into its shell. This is neither accomplishment nor wisdom. Not only is it useless, it bespeaks a pessimistic attitude. Such people feel peaceful, safe, and without worries: "I have found true tranquillity. There is nothing more for me to do." They are reluctant to leave a tranquillity where nothing happens, and try to return to it whenever they meditate. Not only does this fall short of enlightenment, it is not even shallow samadhi. What often happens is that they disassociate from the rest of the world. All they want is to get to the cushion so they can sit in a fog of tranquillity.

Most people come to retreat with seeking minds. They want to gain or attain something. Fortunately, by the time retreat is over, most of them have changed their minds about the purpose of retreats. Or, if their minds did not change, they probably leave disappointed. You are already off to a good start if you come to retreat with a non-seeking mind. Then, whether or not you gain anything good does not matter. The best reason for going on retreat is to practice intensely in an environment suited for that. If you come with a free mind and are not attached to results and outcomes, then nothing can bind you. That alone is reason to feel good.

Even though not enlightened, we can emulate enlightened behavior. Start with not being overly attached to results and benefits. These are all self-centered thoughts. If you succeed, fine; if you fail, fine. Hopefully, such an attitude will extend to your daily life as well. When you cultivate a mind that does not calculate success and failure, your life will be much freer and easier. If you cannot cultivate such an attitude here, where the conditions are right, how can you expect to do so in daily life? If you sit on your cushion comparing your experiences to what you imagine to be others', you are only creating more vexations.

The next two lines, *Whatever it does, there is no obstruction; going and staying are equal,* reiterate the previous lines. When your mind is non-arising and free of all attachments, then you cannot be obstructed; you are free to come and go as you please. In fact, at that point there is no difference between coming and going. Healthy or sick, rich or poor, alive or dead, all are equal to the mind without obstructions or attachments. When the Buddhist sutras speak of the treasure of enlightenment, they are not referring to material wealth, power, or prestige. They are talking about the richness of one whose mind is free. The mind of liberation responds to all situations with equanimity, true wisdom, and compassion, but until we are enlightened, we can practice having a better attitude about gain and loss. So work diligently without calculating success or failure.

12.3 ▪ The Unmoving Wisdom of Enlightenment

> The sun of wisdom is tranquil,
> The light of samadhi is bright.
> Illuminating the garden of no forms,
> Shining on the city of nirvana.

People tell me I must have a lot of wisdom because I have written so many books and have so many students. But writing books and lecturing is intellectual wisdom, not the wisdom of enlightenment, so the wisdom that the *Song* speaks of must be something else.

How does this unmoving wisdom manifest? From where does it come? Some say it is buddha-nature, or total awareness, or that which arises from the unmoving mind. Others do not try to explain it, but compare it to a limitless mirror, or the brightness of an infinite sun. These are vain attempts to explain the inexplicable.

Buddhadharma speaks of two kinds of wisdom—original wisdom and acquired wisdom. Original wisdom is unmoving and is revealed when there are no more discriminations, no more attachments, and no more vexations. Acquired wisdom is wisdom in action; it is the function of original wisdom that responds to sentient beings.

The sun of wisdom is tranquil describes unmoving, original wisdom, which arises when there is no more self to which one attaches. *The light of samadhi is bright* refers to the illuminating function of acquired wisdom. In this case samadhi does not refer to levels of meditative absorption, but rather to the highest samadhi that comes with Chan enlightenment. It is also evident that "tranquil" and "bright" describe different aspects of wisdom.

The next two lines, *Illuminating the garden of no forms, shining on the city of nirvana,* need further clarification. Can a garden with no forms truly exist? Can there be a city of nirvana? I recently visited the Brooklyn Botanical Gardens and walked through British-, French-, and Japanese-style gardens. They even had gardens for the blind, and gardens based on the flowers and herbs mentioned in Shakespeare's plays. Obviously, this is a garden with forms. There would be nothing to do in a garden without forms, yet this is what the *Song* describes. It is impossible for a garden of no forms to exist in the material world, but it can exist in the mind of one who is no longer attached to any forms, whether of the self, others, samsara, or nirvana. In the realm of formlessness, there is no attachment to anything. As we said previously, coming and going are the same. This does not mean that enlightened beings live in a vacuum; they live and act in a world of forms even though their minds reside in the formless realm.

Shining on the city of nirvana is a message to arhats who follow the Hinayana path to self-liberation. Such enlightened beings have uncovered their original wisdom, but if they do not help other sentient beings, acquired wisdom does not function. In fact, the acquired wisdom of bodhisattvas shines on arhats, encouraging them to leave the empty city of nirvana to help sentient beings.

Mahayana Buddhism asserts that the nirvana of self-liberation is not ultimate. It is not the great nirvana that comes to practitioners who follow the bodhisattva path of helping others. We recite the Four Great Vows every day to keep in mind compassion, bodhi mind, and the welfare of sentient beings. However, these principles should not be in your mind when you are actually meditating. Trust that the vows you make will carry over of their own accord, and leave them behind when you sit.

12.4 ▩ When There Are No Thoughts, Who Are You?

> After all relationships are forgotten,
> Spirit is understood and settled in substance.
> Not rising from the Dharma seat,
> Sleeping peacefully in a vacant room.

After all relationships are forgotten speaks of all mental and external phenomena we have encountered, and will encounter. "Forgotten" simply means that the enlightened mind is not attached to, and does not dwell on, such things. This is not to imply there are no longer relationships, nor does it mean that there is no response to phenomena. It means that relating and responding do not disturb the enlightened mind.

Some people fear enlightenment will cause them to forget everything they deem important—loved ones, careers, experiences, points of view. This is not what "forgotten" means. Enlightened beings do not deny the existence of anything, yet they attach to nothing. When you meditate, you can emulate enlightened beings by letting go of your past and your environment. Put down everything until you sit clearly in the present moment. But when there are no wandering thoughts, then who are you? You may think that is enlightenment, but it is not. When all thoughts of past and future are left behind, and you sit clearly in the present moment, there is still an awareness of self—whether small and subtle, or expansive and one with everything, a self-center still exists.

However, such clarity can be considered samadhi. Your awareness of time indicates the depth of your samadhi. If you are in samadhi for a short time but feel that it was a very long time, that would indicate a shallow samadhi. On the other hand, if you are in samadhi for a long time but feel only an instant has elapsed, that shows a deeper level of samadhi. In either case, because there is awareness of time, there is still attachment to a self-center.

Chan does not advocate practicing for samadhi. Conventional Buddha-dharma states that one must experience samadhi before experiencing enlightenment, but Chan asserts that one can directly experience enlightenment without samadhi. *All relationships are forgotten* refers to the mind that directly experiences no-self and leaves behind all attachments, including awareness of time and the present moment.

Spirit is understood and settled in substance means that enlightened beings still actively participate in the world. "Spirit" is the acquired wisdom with which enlightened beings respond to phenomena and sentient beings.

It is said that enlightened beings respond to sentient beings without self-interest. Does this mean that they give sentient beings whatever they want? I have said that the enlightened mind does not discriminate. Does this mean that enlightened persons who make decisions are really *not* enlightened? Suppose seven bachelors propose marriage to an enlightened woman. Each one has good reasons why she should marry him. What should she do? If she wishes to give them what they need, she will have to marry all seven. Of course, she is not getting married for her own sake. If she is enlightened, she has no need to be with anyone. She is simply responding to the needs of others. The answer is that, as an enlightened bodhisattva, her actions would flow from wisdom, and she would decide appropriately. Obviously, what sentient beings think they want or need is not always what they get. Bodhisattvas vow to deliver and help sentient beings; they are not genies who fulfill everyone's wishes.

Not rising from the Dharma seat, sleeping peacefully in a vacant room describes an enlightened bodhisattva's point of view. The best way to help sentient beings is with the wisdom that derives from enlightenment. To use one's body and other physical objects to help others is limited. There is only so much one physical body can do. *Not rising from the Dharma seat* means never leaving the Dharma as one helps sentient beings.

Sleeping peacefully in a vacant room is actually better understood as sleeping peacefully in limitless space. In other words, it does not matter where, when, or how many sentient beings require the help of a bodhisattva. If they have karmic affinity, the bodhisattva will respond. Great bodhisattvas may seem to sentient beings like they have ten thousand arms and eyes, seeing and helping sentient beings everywhere. However, bodhisattvas do not perceive that they are responding at all, as if they were "sleeping peacefully." This is so because bodhisattvas have left behind all relationships and attachments. The *Platform Sutra* says something similar: "When neither hatred nor love disturbs our mind, serenely we sleep."

No Goals for Enlightened Beings

> Taking pleasure in Dao is calming,
> Wandering free and easy in reality.
> No action and nothing to attain,
> Relying on nothing, manifesting naturally.

One who takes pleasure in following the Dao, or path, of Chan lives freely and easily. In doing my part to bring Dharma to people, I have a busy life—writing, lecturing, leading retreats, traveling around the world, overseeing major projects. People tell me that they do not envy my position, but I do not feel any stress, and I take great pleasure in all I do. On the other hand, I see people trying to enjoy what they call vacations, and what I see is tension, frenzy, vexation, and suffering.

Enlightened beings live without bondage or limitation. Even when they appear busy, they are very much at ease. Ordinary people want to get something, but cannot, and wanting to avoid something else, but cannot. They do not realize that what they want to grasp and reject are illusory. But when you have no self-center, there is no need to grasp or reject anything.

No action and nothing to attain, relying on nothing, manifesting naturally means that there are no goals for enlightened beings. They live in the midst of sentient beings, helping naturally, yet with no specific idea or desire to do so. These lines are also valuable advice for Chan practitioners. Once retreat begins, forget whatever purposes you may have had in coming. Whatever you want to attain will only become an obstruction leading to vexation. One of you said to me, "I've been sitting quite well, but I feel I should move on to the next stage. There must be something better than this. How come I'm not moving any higher?" Thoughts like these will guarantee that you will not make progress; in fact, they will likely cause your apparently good state to end.

All you need to do is stick to your method. If you are diligent until the last second of retreat, I guarantee success. Still, you will have attained nothing, and there is really nothing to attain. Only with such an attitude will enlightenment be possible.

12.5 ▦ The Four Unlimited Minds

> The four unlimited minds and the six paramitas
> Are all on the path of one vehicle.
> If mind is not born,
> Dharmas will not differ from one another.

The four unlimited minds—kindness, compassion, joy, and equanimity—are practices of the Hinayana path. The six *paramitas* (perfections)—generosity, morality, patience, diligence, meditation, and wisdom—are practices of the Mahayana path. For a Chan practitioner, they are also practices of the buddha path. I will not go into the similarities and differences between the four unlimited minds and the six *paramitas*, except to say they are all methods of practice. Some might argue the superiority of the Mahayana path because it espouses the bodhisattva ideal. Others might say the Hinayana path is better because it is closer to the original teachings of the Buddha. The enlightened mind does not bother with such distinctions, and neither should Chan practitioners. They are all part of the buddha path.

Some people might think that counting breaths is a beginner's method, whereas *huatou* is an advanced method; or even that sitting meditation is minor Dharma whereas "no practice and no attainment" is major Dharma. This kind of attitude only causes problems, because it feeds the mind that seeks some things and rejects others.

The other day I saw someone warm a bagel in the oven. He then ate part of it, and put the rest in the refrigerator. Later, he took it out and heated it again. I thought, "How can he do that? I would break my teeth trying to bite into that." But, perhaps for someone with sharp teeth and a strong jaw, it would be quite pleasurable. Everyone has different likes and dislikes, different strengths and weaknesses, and different affinities.

When it comes to Chan practice, each person should be given an appropriate method. Furthermore, practitioners should understand that as long as their methods are appropriate, they are the best ones.

It is pointless to consider whether the method you use is good or bad, inferior or superior, minor or major. We should not have such ideas. Some people have practiced breath counting for years and will do so for the rest of their life. I have also known practitioners who have worked on the same *huatou* for their entire lives, and they continue to make progress. Some have even had enlightenment experiences, yet they continue to work on the same *huatou*.

It is even easier to work on a *gong'an* for your entire life and never get bored. *Gong'ans* contain many levels of meaning, some shallow, some deep. Furthermore, there are beginning, intermediate, and advanced *gong'ans*. Some teachers give their students a series of *gong'ans* to work on as their practice deepens. In fact, this is a common practice of many Zen teachers. But it is not necessary. On one hand, you can work on the same *gong'an* and find deeper and more subtle meanings in it as your practice deepens. On the other hand, if you experience deep enlightenment, then all answers to all *gong'ans* instantly become crystal clear to you, so there is no need to work on any others. Of course, this rarely happens.

To enlightened beings, all Dharma is the same. They make no distinctions between good and bad, minor and major. Scholars like to categorize. They separate worldly Dharma from Buddhadharma. Then they distinguish between Hinayana Dharma and Mahayana Dharma. They further separate Mahayana Dharma into gradual enlightenment Dharma and sudden enlightenment Dharma. For enlightened beings, such distinctions are unnecessary. All Dharma is the same.

Functioning in the Midst of Activity

We now come to the final four lines of the *Song of Mind*.

> Knowing arising is non-arising,
> Eternity appears now.

Only the wise understand,
No words can explain enlightenment.

"Non-arising" refers to liberated arhats whose minds are unmoving and
no longer giving rise to any functions. Abiding in nirvana and not help-
ing sentient beings, they do not follow the bodhisattva path. At worst,
they are like lifeless rocks. The minds of deeply enlightened beings still
rise to help others, but are not vexed by anything. Thus, *Knowing arising is
non-arising* describes the mind of wisdom that functions in the midst of
activity, yet remains unmoved.

I have seen practitioners whose bodies became disassociated from
their minds, or their pasts from the present. They may not even recognize
their own bodies or their environment. Their mind still functions, but
they are completely focused on the method in the present moment. They
appear to be sluggish and dull to others. It is not a dangerous situation.
In fact, it is a good sign, and it is a stage that most people must go
through in their practice. However, it is a stage that should not last too
long. If it did, retreats would be taking normal, everyday people and
turning them into zombies. This is not what the *Song of Mind* means by
the mind of wisdom.

Most Chan practitioners are familiar with the following saying: "At
the first stage, mountains are mountains and rivers are rivers. At the sec-
ond stage, mountains are no longer mountains and rivers are no longer
rivers. At the third stage, mountains are again mountains and rivers are
again rivers." Most people spend their entire lives at the first stage, char-
acterized by a self-centered mind, which can discriminate between this
and that, but is vexed by phenomena. The second stage describes deeply
engaged practitioners who are aware only of the present moment, and as
a result are disassociated from their bodies and the environment. People
at this stage may have a difficult time functioning normally. The third
stage describes the enlightened condition. Once again, people are com-
pletely aware of everything around them and can make clear distinctions
between this and that. The difference is that they are no longer attached
to an ego, so they are not moved or vexed by the environment. It is the

mind of wisdom that now responds to the environment. It is the mind of wisdom that the *Song* describes.

Eternity appears now refers to thoroughly enlightened beings. As I said before, the enlightened mind appears to arise because it responds to the environment; but in truth, it does not arise because there is no attachment to a self-center. The enlightened mind has no thoughts that are apart from wisdom. The thoughts of ordinary sentient beings are like ripples on the surface of a pond—transient and discontinuous. The thoughts of the enlightened mind, however, are like the surface of still water, clearly reflecting whatever appears before it, yet remaining undisturbed. Truly, every thought that arises in the enlightened mind is eternal because it is not separate from wisdom.

This is something only the enlightened can understand, for no words can explain enlightenment. To them, explanations are unnecessary anyway. In other words, everything I have said is really not true. They are not wisdom, only words. True understanding only comes with direct experience. These lectures, the Buddhist sutras, shastras, songs, poems, and commentaries are useful only insofar as they encourage you to practice and incorporate the Dharma into your daily life. If your interest is purely intellectual, then the words are useless and empty. It is my hope that they inspire you to practice, because the only knowledge that is worthwhile is that which you experience yourself. True wisdom is revealed only upon enlightenment.

Glossary

Abbreviations: C. = Chinese, J. = Japanese, S. = Sanskrit

Arhat: (S., lit. "worthy one") One who has experienced personal liberation, and thus attained nirvana. The arhat has accomplished the path, and, in that sense, has "no more to learn," has extinguished all passions, and will not again enter the cycle of birth and death (samsara). See Bodhisattva.

Bhumi: (S., lit. "land" or "ground") One of the ten stages of the bodhisattva path leading to complete enlightenment as a buddha. The first stage is the arousal of the aspiration to enlightenment by practicing the bodhisattva path. Each successive stage takes the bodhisattva to more and more complete enlightenment, until the ninth, in which wisdom is fully developed. The tenth stage is the attainment of full buddhahood. Shakyamuni, the buddha of our era, is understood to have attained the tenth *bhumi*.

Bodhi: (S., lit. "awakened") The awakened or enlightened state.

Bodhidharma: Indian monk, ca. 470-543 CE, considered to be the 28th patriarch of Indian Buddhism and the first patriarch of Chinese Chan Buddhism. Bodhidharma was notable for his emphasis on the practice of dhyana (meditation) as a means of directly realizing enlightenment.

Bodhisattva: (S., lit. "awakened being") The bodhisattva, the ideal of the Mahayana school of Buddhism, practices for the sake of helping sentient beings as opposed to one's own liberation. In this sense, the bodhisattva path is often contrasted with that of the arhat. *See* Arhat.

Buddhadharma: (S., lit. "truth, or law, of the Buddha") The teachings of Buddhism as espoused by the historical Buddha, who was born in India as Siddhartha Gotama of the Shakya clan, circa 563 BCE. He was later given the honorific of Shakyamuni ("sage of the Shakya clan"), and was called the Buddha ("awakened one") after he achieved enlightenment. He is referred to as Shakyamuni Buddha to distinguish him from other Buddhas. Collectively, Buddhadharma consists of the teachings of the Buddha in the form of the Buddhist canon—the sutras attributed to the Buddha—the Nikayas (Pali canon) and the Agamas (Sanskrit canon).

Buddha-mind: The enlightened mind of the Buddha, also referred to as "bodhi mind" or "self-nature."

Caodong: (J., Soto) One of the two major surviving sects of Chan Buddhism, the other being the Linji (J., Rinzai). Like the Linji sect, Caodong espouses sudden enlightenment, but with greater emphasis on the practice of silent illumination, as opposed to the *gong'an* and *huatou* practice of the Linji sect. See Linji.

Dharma: In Buddhist philosophy "dharma" has two contexts. One context is often spelled in English with a capital "D" to refer to the teachings of the Buddha, also known as "Buddhadharma." The second context is used in English with a lowercase "d" to refer to phenomenon, whether mental or external.

Dharmadhatu: (S., lit. "realm of dharma") The realm in which all phenomena (dharmas) arise, abide, and disappear. As such it represents the true nature of all things.

Dharmakaya: (S., lit. "dharma body") *See* Trikaya.

Dhyana: (S., lit. "meditative absorption") "Dhyana" is the Sanskrit word of which the Chinese "Chan" and the Japanese "Zen" are transliterations. "Dhyana" traditionally designates the meditative absorption in order to liberate oneself from mental defilements. In Chan/Zen, however, "dhyana" has a different connotation, and refers to the method of cultivating the mind towards directly realizing enlightenment.

Five Hellish Deeds: The Five Hellish Deeds are: (1) matricide, (2) patricide, (3) murder of an arhat, (4) injury of a buddha, and (5) attempting to bring about a schism in the Buddhist monastic community.

Five Hindrances: The Five Hindrances are: (1) desire, (2) ill will, (3) sloth and torpor, (4) restlessness and anxiety, and (5) doubt. The hindrances are obstructions that prevent practitioners from attaining concentration and meditative absorption.

Five Methods for Stilling the Mind: Group of meditative methods consisting of: (1) mindfulness of breath, (2) contemplating the impurity of the body, (3) mindful recollection of the buddhas and bodhisattvas, (4) meditation on the four limitless mentalities (loving-kindness, compassion, joy, equanimity), and (5) contemplating causes and conditions.

Five Precepts: The five precepts are: (1) not to kill, (2) not to steal, (3) not to lie, (4) not to commit sexual misconduct, and (5) not to take intoxicants.

Four Great Vows: The four vows of the bodhisattva are: (1) I vow to deliver innumerable sentient beings, (2) I vow to eradicate all vexations, (3) I vow to master limitless approaches to Dharma, (4) I vow to attain supreme buddhahood.

Four Noble Truths: The Four Noble Truths are the foundation teaching of all Buddhism, expounded by Shakyamuni Buddha at the first sermon following his enlightenment. The Four Noble Truths are: (1) the existence of suffering, (2) the origin of suffering, (3) that there is a way out of suffering, and (4) the cessation of suffering through the Eightfold Noble Path, which consists of: right view, right thought, right speech, right action, right livelihood, right effort, right mindfulness, and right meditation.

Gong'an: (C., pronounced GOONG-ahn; lit. "public case") Method of practice used in Chan and Zen Schools in which the practitioner intensely "investigates" a historical saying, dialogue, or event, often between a Chan master and a disciple. The purpose is to concentrate on the *gong'an* to the exclusion of all other thoughts, thus making possible the raising of the "great doubt." *See Huatou*, Koan.

Heart Sutra: English title of the *Mahaprajnaparamita Hridaya Sutra*, the best-known of the Mahayana sutras, which proclaims "emptiness" as the fundamental characteristic of phenomena, including that of the "self."

Huatou: (C.; J. *wato*, lit. "head of a thought") Chan and Zen method of meditation that uses a question or fragment from a *gong'an* to "investigate" its meaning. In Chan and Zen, *huatou* is often used interchangeably with gong'an. *See also* Gong'an, Koan.

Huineng (638–713): Dajian Huineng (J. Daikan Eno) was the sixth patriarch of the Chan lineage, and is considered to be the founder of the "sudden enlightenment" tradition of Chan. As a young monk, he became enlightened when he heard someone recite from the *Diamond Sutra*.

Incense Board: A flat stick (*kyosaku* in Zen) traditionally used by Chan and Zen teachers to strike the shoulder(s) of meditating students to spur them on to greater effort, and in some cases, to provoke awakening.

Klesa: (S., lit. "defilement, passion") *Klesas* are the impurities of the deluded mind, chiefly greed, aversion, and delusion (ignorance) that together are known as the "three poisons." One formulation consists of ten *klesas*—the three above, plus pride, false views, doubt, rigidity, excitability, shamelessness, and lack of conscience.

Koan: (J., transliteration of the Chinese "*gong'an*.") *See Gong'an*.

Linji (d. 866): Master Linji (J. Rinzai) was the founder of the sect of Chan Buddhism that bears his name. The Linji sect was characterized by its emphasis on meditation and the use of gong'an and *huatou* to create a "doubt mass" in the mind of the practitioner. The resolution of the doubt mass is an essential step toward realizing "self-nature," or enlightenment. The Linji sect is one of two major surviving Chan sects, the other being the Caodong. *See also* Caodong.

Nirmanakaya: (S., lit. "transformation body.") *See* Trikaya.

Nirvana: (S., lit. "extinction") State of liberation from samsara (the cycle of birth and death); it is the cessation of suffering and its arising, and is entered when one has overcome all attachments and is free from all karma. *See also* Samsara.

Paramita: (S., lit. "having reached the other shore") Often translated as "perfection," a *paramita* is a virtue or practice perfected by practitioners on the Buddhist path. The six *paramitas* are practices for all followers of the path: (1) generosity, (2) morality or discipline, (3) patience, (4) diligence, (5) meditation, and (6) wisdom. The Ten *Paramitas* are the practices of bodhisattvas, and consist of the six *paramitas*, plus (7) right means, (8) vows, (9) manifestation of the ten powers, and (10) true knowledge of dharmas (phenomena).

Patriarchs: In Chan Buddhism, "patriarch" refers to one of the six teachers in succession who are considered to be the "founding fathers" of Chan (Zen). The first patriarch was Bodhidharma (d. circa 536), the Indian monk who went to China in the sixth century CE. The line of succession after Bodhidharma consists of Dazu Huike (487–593), Jianzhi Sengcan (d. 606), Dayi Daoxin (580–651), Daman Hongren (602–675), and Dajian Huineng (638–713).

Pratyekabuddha: (S., lit. "solitary awakened one") A self-enlightened being who gained that status through insight into the process of dependent origination.

Pure Land: The Land of Supreme Bliss, or the Western Paradise of Amitabha Buddha. It is a pure realm that came into existence due to the vows of Amitabha Buddha. Anyone who sincerely invokes Amitabha's name and expresses the wish to be born there will be reborn in the Pure Land.

Samboghakaya: (S., lit. "body of delight.") *See* Trikaya.

Samsara: (S., lit. "journeying") The cycle of birth and death that a sentient being experiences until no new karma is created and all karma has been extinguished, at which point one enters nirvana. *See also* Nirvana.

Shastra: (S., lit. "instruction") A commentary or treatise on Buddhist doctrine, often based on one of the Buddha's sutras. *See* Sutra.

Shifu: (C.) Honorific for "teacher."

Shikantaza: The Japanese Zen meditation practice that is similar to the silent illumination of Caodong Chan. Used in the Soto School, its main feature is sitting in meditation with only the awareness of oneself sitting in meditation.

Six Paramitas: *See* Paramita.

Skandhas, The Five: (S., lit. "heaps" or "aggregates") The *skandhas* are the five constituent factors that make up the conscious life of a sentient being, leading to development of the illusion of independent existence and possession of a "self." They are form, sensation, perception, volition, and consciousness. The first *skandha*, form, is physical in nature, while the remaining four are mental.

Sutra: (S., lit. "instruction") A commentary or treatise on Buddhist doctrine, often based on one of the Buddha's sutras. *See* Shastra.

Ten Evil Deeds: The Ten Evil Deeds, the opposite of the Ten Virtuous Deeds, are: (1) killing; (2) stealing; (3) committing adultery; (4) lying; (5) double tonguing (hypocrisy); (6) using coarse language; (7) using harsh language; (8) coveting; (9) being angry; (10) holding perverted views.

Ten Virtuous Deeds: The Ten Virtuous Deeds, the opposite of the Ten Evil Deeds, are: (1) not killing, (2) not stealing, (3) not committing adultery, (4) not lying, (5) not double tonguing (hypocrisy), (6) not using coarse language, (7) not using filthy language, (8) not coveting, (9) not being angry, and (10) not holding perverted views.

Trikaya: (S., lit. "three bodies") The *trikaya* is the Mahayana belief in the threefold nature of a fully realized buddha, consisting of *dharmakaya*, *sambhogakaya*, and *nirmanakaya*. The *dharmakaya* (lit. "body of the truth, or law") is the transcendent body of the buddhas, perfect and devoid of characteristics. There are different interpretations of the second and third bodies. One common interpretation is that the *sambhogakaya* (lit. "body of delight") is the accumulated result, or retribution, of the buddha's merit, and is an object of devotion. The *nirmanakaya* (lit. "body of transformation") is the incarnated form of a buddha who has chosen to return to help sentient beings.

Twelve Links of Conditioned Arising: The twelve links, or stages (S. *nidanas*), traversed by a sentient being in the cycle of birth and death (samsara). Together these links constitute an unbroken chain of causes and conditions that lead to further stages in the cycle of "conditioned arising." The links are: (1) ignorance, (2) action, (3) consciousness, (4) name-and-form, (5) the six sense faculties, (6) contact, (7) sensation, (8) craving, (9) grasping, (10) becoming, (11) birth, (12) old age and death.

Printed in the United States
By Bookmasters